PELICAN BOOKS

A 472

INVITATION TO PILGRIMAGE

JOHN BAILLIE

JOHN BAILLIE

Invitation to Pilgrimage

PENGUIN BOOKS

Penguin Books Ltd, Harmondsworth, Middlesex
AUSTRALIA: Penguin Books Pty Ltd, 762 Whitehorse Road,
Mitcham, Victoria

—

First published by the Oxford University Press 1942
Published in Pelican Books 1960

Made and printed in Great Britain
by William Clowes and Sons, Limited
London and Beccles

Contents

Preface

The following pages represent the Alexander Robertson Lectures which were delivered in the University of Glasgow in the Summer Term of last year. It is prescribed that the lectures shall be 'in defence of the Christian religion', and I thought it right to follow this prescription closely. Addressing myself to all earnest seekers after truth, I have sought to give them good reason why they should follow the Christian Way.

Some parts of the book may also, if they chance upon them, be recognized as familiar by those who attended any of the various other short courses of lectures which I had the privilege of delivering during the year – in Princeton, New Jersey, in February; to the Conference of the Student Christian Movement at St Andrews in July; and to undergraduates in the Universities of both Glasgow and Edinburgh during the Autumn Term.

I wish to express my thanks to the Court of the University of Glasgow for the honour they did me in appointing me to the Alexander Robertson Lectureship. I have also gratefully to acknowledge the great help afforded me in the revision of the proofs by my friend, the Rev. J. Y. Campbell, M.A., of Kilmacolm, and by my brother, the Rev. Professor D. M. Baillie, D.D., of the University of St Andrews.

JOHN BAILLIE

EDINBURGH
January 1942

I

The Fork in the Road

THE invitation has come to me to say what I can, within the limits of these few lectures which are afterwards to be published in the form of a book, 'in defence of the Christian religion'. However great my feeling of my own inadequacy in face of so responsible a task, I cannot deny that the invitation is in itself a reasonable one. I number among my own friends and acquaintances and colleagues and associates not a few men and women who stand aloof from the fellowship of the Christian Church and think that they have good reason for so doing, and I know well that it is my duty to join friendly issue with them as often as opportunity arises, 'being always ready with an *apologia* for every one who asks of you a reason concerning the hope which is in you – but with gentleness and due deference'.[1] I know also that from the very beginning, and even before the days of the Roman persecution from which that injunction dates, my fellow Christians were called upon to offer an *apologia* for their faith and responded nobly to the demand. 'From the beginning', writes an eminent scholar, 'our religion has been called on to defend itself against misunderstandings and bitter opposition.... It may be accepted as one of the most certain results of modern criticism that the New Testament is permeated with an apologetic interest which is often strongest when it is least apparent.'[2]

1. 1 Peter 3:15. The word I render as deference, and which I might almost have rendered as diffidence, is φόβος which is thus defined in its New Testament usage by Souter, *A Pocket Lexicon to the Greek New Testament*: '*fear, terror*, often fear on the reverential side, in reference to God, and such as inspires cautious dealing towards men. cf. 1 Peter i, 17.'

2. E. F. Scott, *The Apologetic of the New Testament*, p. 2 f.

There is, however, an important difference between the situation in which these early Christian apologists found themselves and that in which I am now placed. The apologetic of the New Testament, and of the early centuries generally, was addressed to men who had been brought up within one or other of the great pre-Christian religious systems and who staunchly defended their own inherited traditions against the innovation of the Christian outlook; whereas any apologetic that is to be effective in this country today must be addressed to men who stand within the inheritance of the *Christian* tradition and know nothing, save by hearsay, of any other, but who have now in varying degrees disengaged themselves from this tradition and whose quarrel with Christianity is therefore undertaken from the point of view either of no religion at all or of some very vague and tenuous residuum of Christian religiosity – or, it may be, of some tentative new-conceived substitute for it. Such is the spiritual situation of not a few men and women with whom it has been my lot, and in many ways also my privilege, to associate almost daily; and not least of many who have been or now are my colleagues in one or other of the several seats of learning where I have been appointed to profess the Christian doctrine. And such is obviously the situation to which my present argument must in the first place be addressed.

What is my argument to be, then? What can I say that is likely to commend the Christian faith in which I stand to those of my contemporaries who have thus lost their hold upon it? It seems to me that in the last resort there is only one thing I can do, and that is to attempt to illuminate the point or points of divergence between their outlook and my own. They and I have very much in common. If we had nothing in common, there would be nothing I could say to them. Speech cannot proceed except on the basis of some measure of understanding between the speakers. Argument cannot begin except from some major premise the truth of which is acknowledged by both parties. Actually, however, there is a long stretch of road that we are accustomed to walk together before we reach the parting of the ways. About many things my dissenting friends think and feel very much as I do. To many of life's alarms they respond very much as I do. Their outlook on large areas of our common environment is very much the same. Or perhaps it is rather that in our outlook on *everything*, in our response to *all* life's alarms, there is something that we have in common and again something that divides us. And I am sure that the bit of the road that most requires to be illuminated is the point where it forks. If we could only discover just why it is that, when a certain stage is reached, we take different turnings and begin to walk apart, we should perhaps be doing all that we can humanly do. The rest is not in our hands, but in the hands of Something or Some One not ourselves; for faith is not an achievement but a gift. The unbeliever cannot force himself to believe, and the believer, so far as he believes, cannot help believing. But if the final issue is in other hands, I am sure it is in much better hands, and that all will be well in the end if only we play valiantly the small part that is alone open to us.

We cannot, however, find where the roads forks without first illuminating the road itself. Our searchlight must follow the road up to the parting, and then for some distance beyond it along the divergent ways. We can understand the precise nature of the difference between us only after we have first understood what we believe in common, and then the nature of our further belief and unbelief. And yet the road would stand much less in need of illumination if there was no fork in it. If we all had the same belief, there would be much less urgency to understand what we believe. It is only divergency of belief that ever forces belief to be self-conscious. Those human societies which enjoy an unbroken uniformity of spiritual outlook have never formulated any such thing as a creed; they believe, but they have never reflected on their beliefs, and they are not even aware of the determinative part which beliefs of any kind play in the shaping of their lives. It is a commonplace that all the Christian creeds, and not least the Apostles' Creed, were first put together in an apologetic interest. It is well known also that it was the rise of heresy within the Christian Church that occasioned the formulation of Christian dogma. The history of dogma is a history of choices taken between alternative ways of belief that had already made their appearance within the Church, and no dogma has ever been defined until some considerable body of opinion had doubted that which it concerned itself to affirm. It is the heretics who have forced the Church to clear its mind, but whenever heresy has appeared, or rather whenever an important division of opinion has appeared (for no opinion becomes a heresy until a dogma has already been defined against it, so that if in one sense it is heresy that creates dogma, in another it is dogma that creats heresy), the Church has then made haste to clear its mind as best it could. As was said by St Anselm, our great Archbishop of the eleventh century, 'Just as the right order of going requires that we should believe the deep things of God before we presume to discuss them by reason, so it seems to me negligence if, after we have been confirmed in the faith, we do *not* study to understand what we believe.'[1] These words may be taken as the charter of our present little enterprise. And yet it is clear that I must study to understand not only my own belief but also the attitude of mind of those who believe differently or do not believe at all. It is perhaps even more important for the unbeliever to know what and why he does not believe than it is for the believer to know what and why he believes. There are two things, then, that I must do, if I am to throw any helpful illumination upon the fork in the road – I must make plain the nature of the belief of those who believe and the nature of the unbelief of those who do not believe. That, of course, is to talk largely, for it is

1. *Cur deus homo*, Cap. I.

obvious that I lack both the ability and the present opportunity
to do more than nibble at so vast and perennial a problem. But
I mean only to define my conception of the essential nature of
the task to which one who briefly speaks or writes 'in
defence of the Christian religion' must bring in his exiguous
contribution.

2

The By-way of Unbelief

I HAVE no doubt whatever that St Anselm's words *intelligere quod credimus*, with the addition of *quod non credimus* – 'to understand what we believe and what we do not believe' – lead us right to the heart of the problem. I have no doubt that difficulties of belief are immensely complicated and aggravated by misunderstanding. Of course, they are never due to misunderstanding alone; another factor is always concerned in them, namely, sin; and it is this hopelessly ravelled and reticulated tangle of sin and unreason, of wrong motives and wrong logic, coming from a bad heart and a bad head, that creates the real complexity of our task. There can indeed be ignorance without sin; for no finite being, however sinless, could be omniscient. But ignorance is not the same thing as error, and that there can be error without sin is by no means so clear. All who have faith in God must at least agree that in a perfectly sinless soul there could be no such error as would itself alone be sufficient utterly to destroy that faith. The vision of God cannot be shut out from our lives by wrong thinking only, unaccompanied by wrong living. At all events, you and I know nothing about wrong thinking that is unaccompanied by wrong living. All our actual thinking is tainted with sin. Some would indeed have us believe that it is *altogether* the servant of sin. This view is taught in many of the documents of early Protestantism, as for instance in the Westminster Confession of Faith, where we read that our first parents became 'wholly defiled in all the faculties and parts of soul and body', and that this totally corrupted nature was so 'conveyed to all their posterity' that all men are now 'utterly indisposed, disabled, and made opposite to all good, and wholly inclined to all evil'.[1] And there are many contemporary voices that seem to be preaching virtually the same doctrine, though from a very different platform. Both Freud and Marx, the two modern prophets who have probably affected the mind of our time more profoundly than any others, are often found writing as if corrupt desires fathered *all* our thoughts. According to the former our reasoning is mostly rationalization; according to the latter our ideas are mostly ideologies. 'In every epoch', writes the latter, 'the ruling ideas have been the ideas of the ruling class.'[2] For myself, I feel bound to reject such extreme doctrines of total corruption as over-simplifying the issue and doing violence to the existing complexity of human nature, but they are all much nearer the truth than most of us care to admit, and also much nearer the truth than are the contrary ideas against which they were directed. I hope I have learned something from each of them which has been of help to me in my own confession of sin. Wrong belief is always mixed with wrong desire. But – and this is my present point – right belief is always mixed with wrong desire too, since all human states of mind are mixed with wrong desire. Therefore what determines one man wrongly to disbelieve what another rightly believes may not be the greater corruption of his desires but the lesser competence and range and clarity of his thoughts.

That then is what we mean when we say that difficulties of belief are due in large part to misunderstanding, and that the way to defeat this misunderstanding is to study better to comprehend what and why we believe and what and why we disbelieve. It has been my own lot to be constantly involved in discussion with men who feel unable to identify themselves with the faith and outlook of the Christian Church – some of these fancying themselves to be completely out of sympathy

1. Chapter vi, §§ 2–4.
2. Quoted by Sidney Hook, *Towards the Understanding of Karl Marx*, London (1933), p. 121.

with Christianity, others finding difficulty at only one or two vital points. And it is seldom, if ever, that I have felt their doubts and denials to be based upon a true comprehension of what they were doubting and denying, or upon a true comprehension of the opposite platform from which their doubts and denials proceeded, or upon a sufficient illumination of the real point of issue. It is extraordinary how widely the modern world has forgotten what Christianity really is. It has to be confessed that the reproach of the situation must lie in no small part on the Christian Church itself – or rather on those who represent it in the contemporary world. Our Christian witness has been both divided and confused. And too often the witness of our faith and of our deeds has been not one witness but two. 'Is it not unspeakably sad', writes Karl Adam of Tübingen, one of the leading Roman Catholic teachers of our day, 'that we Catholics are no longer, as formerly, recognized by our love, that no longer faith and love, but faith alone is our distinguishing mark?'[1] And faith without works is as dead in its power of testimony as in its power unto salvation. I am quite sure that whenever the sower of the Christian seed finds that what he sows is failing to take root in the world about him, his first thought must be for the defects in his own sowing, and only his second thought for the stoniness of the soil. No Christian teacher can look into his own heart and deny that, where he has failed, a purer and more fully consecrated spirit than his own would in all human likelihood have succeeded.

And yet he must consider the stoniness of the soil also. It is not only because our Christian witness is defective that the true nature of the Christian religion is so largely misconceived in our time. It is also because many men criticize and even oppose Christianity without ever having taken much trouble to discover what it is all about. One might have thought that by this time of day the Christian teaching had received suffi-

1. *Two Essays*, English Translation, London and New York (1930), p. 77.

cient advertisement for educated men to avoid at least the most elementary mistakes in their references to it, but such apparently is not the case. It is remarkable what nonsense is spoken about it even by men of the highest distinction in departmental fields of knowledge. I have myself heard the most astounding nonsense about it from the lips of scholars at whose feet I have willingly sat in the endeavour to acquire a little knowledge in some of these fields (though indeed I must not say this without humility, because I know that my own talking about Christianity has by no means always been informed with good sense). Only the other day I read a book written in direct opposition to Christianity by a very clever woman, some of whose gifts of expression I found myself greatly envying, and yet I closed the book with the unrepentant feeling that hardly a page of it could possibly survive the submission of so alert and fundamentally honest a mind to an elementary course of instruction in any theological college. And how often I feel the same thing in reading our contemporary novels! Few of our high-brow novelists – and they are so very high-brow nowadays! – can leave religion alone, but their references to it are often quite pitiful in their crudity. Recently a friend of mine was sitting quietly by my fireside, reading a novel which I had lent him, when I was startled to see him violently fling down the book (which had cost me good money and which I had bought because everybody was reading it) and exclaim, 'I often think that some of these modern novelists have never met a good man – or even a nice woman!' At least one often wonders whether they have ever seen anything like Christian saintliness at anything like first hand; and especially whether they have ever seen the inside of a Christian home. For actually it is very difficult to know what Christianity is unless one has had some intimate knowledge of Christian family life – of the attitude of a Christian husband and wife towards one another and of Christian brothers and sisters towards one another and of Christian parents towards their children. My old teacher, Wilhelm Herrmann of Marburg, used to say that the atmosphere of the Christian household was an almost necessary commentary on the Bible, without which it must be very difficult indeed for a modern man to interpret these ancient writings. 'When we live in the midst of Christian people', he writes in one of his books, 'the sense is awakened by which we may see God in Christ, and the germ of understanding is nourished.'[1] And again he writes that in childhood 'we were brought near to God, not by the mere instruction we received in Christian thoughts, but by that personal life sanctified of God which found expression in the instruction.'[2] In spite of all that may and must be said about the 'remaining corruption' of human nature even in the souls of the saints, I have myself been privileged to see shining examples of household Christianity such as must have melted a heart of stone. Nor would I have it thought that there are not also many novels in which the Christian temper is truly revealed – from O. Douglas's *The Setons*, which is no doubt very small beer, though it happens to be about life in Glasgow, all the way up to Dostoyevsky's *The Brothers Karamazov* which is about life in Russia and is as strong and spirituous as its vodka.

It is, however, not only the Christian outlook that is subject to misunderstanding but also the possible alternatives to it. How seldom has unbelief really understood its own nature! How seldom are we able to feel, in reading the works of those moderns who have forsaken the Christian outlook, that they have radically examined and tested the contrary platform on which they themselves stand and from which their dissatisfaction and criticism expresses itself! I remember well how during my study of philosophy as an undergraduate one of my teachers wrote the following words (or their like) on the mar-

1. *The Communion of the Christian with God*, Third English edition (1909), p. 190.
2. *Ibid.*, p. 118.

gin of an essay in which I had criticized a certain accepted theory: 'Every theory has its difficulties, but you have not considered whether any other theory has less difficulties than the one you have criticized.' And I remember that the further reflection set up in my mind by that simple remark was, in that particular instance, enough to lead me back to the received doctrine. I am happy to count among my own friends a rather remarkable number of men of high intellectual distinction who have returned to the full Christian outlook after years of defection from it, and I should say that in practically every case the renewed hospitality of their minds to Christian truth came about through their awakening to the essential untenability of the alternative positions which they had been previously attempting to occupy. Their apostasy needed only to become robustly self-critical in order to lose all its conviction. Having examined the ground on which they were standing, they found it to be the veriest marshland or, in the slightly different figure made so familiar by Mr Eliot's poem, to be the veriest 'Waste Land'.

> Here is no water but only rock
> Rock and no water and the sandy road
> The road winding above among the mountains
> Which are mountains of rock without water
> If there were water we should stop and drink
> Amongst the rock one cannot stop or think
> Sweat is dry and feet are in the sand
> If there were only water amongst the rock....[1]

And many who have not yet returned are beginning to be filled with the same sense of desolation. They are not yet convinced that there is better going on the strait and narrow way of the Christian pilgrim's progress than through any of the wide tracts surrounding it on either hand, but they are at least beginning to feel that they have lost their bearings. In many ways indifference to organized Christianity may seem to be

[1]. *The Waste Land*, V.

increasing in our time, yet the intellectual opposition to Christianity is now much less sure of itself than it was a generation ago. The camp-followers of unbelief may be gaining in assurance, but the leaders are beginning to look wistful. It was much easier to define a tenable alternative to Christianity in the nineteenth century than it is today. Unbelief could then put up such a case as it had seldom been able to do before and as it is certainly not able to do now. Especially since the period of the war of 1914–18 its most trusted supports have appeared to crumble. I remember, for instance, how difficult I found it in my own undergraduate days to escape the impressive logic of mechanistic materialism; but where is that logic today? No doubt there are many who attempt to re-edit it in conformity with the changed scientific outlook, but it must be confessed that none of these new editions wears anything like the appearance of impregnability of which the nineteenth-century one could boast. The same is true of the nineteenth-century belief in evolutionary progress, which was built into so imposing a philosophic edifice by Herbert Spencer and many of his contemporaries. Progress, writes Spencer, 'is due to the working of a universal law; ... in virtue of that law it must continue until the state we call perfection is reached.... Thus the ultimate development of the ideal man is logically certain – as certain as any conclusion in which we place the most implicit faith; ... so surely must the things we call evil and immorality disappear; so surely must man become perfect.'[1] Now obviously, if we had been able to go on believing that, it were absurd to trouble about any return to the Christian outlook. Why worry about an Incarnation and an Atonement, why worry even about a God, if we could become ideally good and happy without any of these things? But alack! alack! what has happened to the car of progress today? What kobolds have been tampering with the teeth of its ascending track, sending it hurtling into the abyss? Has any great system of philosophy

1. *Social Statics*, p. 78 f.

ever passed more quickly and more completely into the melancholy archives of the past than Spencer's Synthetic Philosophy, as he chose to call the strange invention? It was to be a system for all time, but who reads in it after fifty years?

The same might be said of the great humanistic system of Auguste Comte which seemed so much alive to a thinker like John Stuart Mill and even to Matthew Arnold. How hard has humanism recently been put to it, in the attempt to maintain its case! The following words are taken from a copy of *The Times Literary Supplement* dating from the year 1934: 'The fundamental ground upon which humanism was negativing Christianity, that man had risen from the dust and was rapidly approaching perfection, has proved mere marshland, and the structure reared upon it has fallen.' Wherever men can now hope to find a solid standing-ground outside Christianity, surely it is not here! Whatever alternative worship they propose, surely they cannot any longer worship man! I remember hearing a great scholar say once that he thought the worship of the sun would be a much healthier alternative. The sun, he said, is a most magnificent object; it is very high up and would at least teach us to look above the level of our own eyes; it is also something not ourselves and would save us from our recent nauseating orgy of self-congratulation. At the time I took that almost as a jest; but the event has forced me to take it seriously. For it is undoubtedly in this general direction that much modern humanism is now tending to lose its identity – in the direction of a relapse into the old paganisms that preceded the advent, not only of Christianity, but of all the great religious systems of the higher pre-Christian civilizations. A similar fate seems to be overtaking still another of the notable alternatives to Christianity which were offered to us by the nineteenth century, namely, communism in the sense of the historical materialism of Karl Marx. Possibly this failure has been the latest to become apparent. The principles of Marxism shone in their day as a bright light for the guidance and comfort of many honest souls, providing them with a prospect that at first seemed not ill founded and that looked like a very fair substitute for the Christian hope. But now the vision of this 'brave new world' has manywise faded. Communism is losing its old conviction, and for more and more of its former champions it is becoming 'the god that failed'. Thus it is clear that a pitiless self-criticism of its own position is no less necessary than a proper understanding of the Christian position, if unbelief is to find its way back to the faith. It is clearly also an immensely important part of the Christian apologist's task that he should assist such unbelief to a more realistic awareness of its own nature.

One thing, however, which the apologist must always have in mind is that the debate between belief and unbelief is by no means merely a debate between himself who believes and another who disbelieves. It is also in large part a debate within himself, who both believes and disbelieves, and who must ever continue to pray humbly, 'Lord, I believe; help thou mine unbelief.' When we who are within the visible Church of Christ reason with those who are without, we are never in the position of feeling that there is in our interlocutors no disposition to believe and in ourselves no disposition to doubt. In saying this, we must not indeed forget Newman's famous statement that 'From the time that I became a Catholic ... I have never had one doubt.'[1] But Newman had at least previously known doubt in his own person, so that in arguing against it, he was arguing against his own previous mind. We others are, however, less fortunate, we still do not find faith altogether easy, and hence our *apologia* is always in some sort addressed to ourselves as well as to our neighbours. The history of Christian thought goes far to confirm this. Very many of the great defences of the faith have been constructed by men who were obviously arguing with their own doubts and difficulties, whether past (because the answer had already been

1. *Apologia pro Vita Sua*, Chapter V.

found) or present (because the answer was only now being worked out with labour and tears); and in constructing them they were as much concerned to fortify their own souls as to confound their adversaries. Seldom has a Christian affirmation been effectively defended by one who had no personal feeling for the difficulty of maintaining it and the force of the exception which might be taken to it. The most moving and persuasive arguments are always those in which the arguer is felt to be holding high debate with himself. Indeed, where this element is altogether wanting, the argument is likely – in such a sphere as religion – to turn out something worse than useless. Mere polemic seldom does anything but stiffen the adversary's resistance. At all events, such argument as will here be offered is argument which the arguer has often, and perforce, had to hold with his own soul. When one looks back over the road oneself has travelled, anything like dogmatism appears very much out of place; anything also like a fencing method or a parade of dialectical skill or the desire to score merely a plausible victory over the opponent.

3

The Constraint of Truth

WHAT the Christian must do, then, in attempting to defend the faith against his own and his neighbours' unbelief is to bring to bear upon the issue the strongest and most merciless possible illumination, so that both faith and unbelief shall be clearly shown up for what they are. Those who are declared enemies of the faith are indeed accustomed to hint, and sometimes they do much more than hint, that any attempt at such illumination would be a grave indiscretion on the part of believers. Our faith, they tell us, will not stand it. It needs only to be pulled out into the open to wither completely away. For, to vary the metaphor, the cat would be out of the bag. Such a challenge the Christian apologist takes up most fearlessly. Indeed he must needs rejoice in it. For, as I have already said, it is in complete honesty and pitiless self-criticism that he finds the world's only hope. He is convinced that it is when all our human cards are on the table that Christ gets his real opportunity. If the apologist is not so convinced, he is not a true Christian believer. For of course, what really matters, and what the true believer has most deeply at heart, is not orthodoxy or conformity but just truth itself.

God, that is to say, must take all the risks of honest inquiry. Yet 'must' is not here the appropriate word, since there is no risk. He is more anxious to take, if only it were ever offered to Him. 'Behold, thou desirest truth in the inward parts.'[1] That is what He desires and what we so seldom give Him. The one great difficulty which confronts God in His desire to reveal Himself to you and me, that thereby He may save us, is the difficulty of cutting through the dreadful tangle

1. Psalm 51 : 6.

of dishonesty and lying self-deception and pathetic make-believe with which we all the time surround ourselves. It would not be quite so bad if we only pretended to others, but alas! we are all the time pretending to ourselves also, and to pretend to oneself is at the same time to pretend to God. '*Chaque homme*', a shrewd Frenchman said, '*a trois caractères: celui qu'il a, celui qu'il montre, et celui qu'il croit avoir.*' And through all this preposterous *étalage* God has to cut His way before He can reach man's real self. True thinking can take place only in the contact between the naked mind and the naked reality which confronts it. If God be really Truth, then in that contact lies His perfect opportunity. But how often is it offered to Him?

Within the modern world since the Renaissance the love of truth has often seemed to lead men away from God. Some of the reasons for this will be before us at a later point in our discussion, but meanwhile one thing may be said. The love of truth is not a sentiment that can properly exist in isolation, apart from all other loves. We hear much nowadays of pure scientific curiosity and of truth for truth's sake, just as in other quarters we hear (or until lately used to hear) of the pure love of beauty and of art for art's sake. But it is psychologically more than doubtful whether curiosity is ever found in its pure state or whether there can be such a thing as the love of truth merely for truth's sake in the abstract sense that is here intended; whether, that is, there can be such a thing as entirely presuppositionless inquiry, *voraussetzungslose Wissenschaft*. What is required of us is not that we should have no presuppositions but that we should have the right ones – that our prejudgements should not be private prejudices. When we think we are moved merely by curiosity, our curiosity is always set in motion by something other than itself; and this is as it should be, if only that other thing be something good. For truth is only one of God's attributes, just as beauty is; and we cannot be saved from an idolatrous corruption of this attribute except we love Him also under His other attributes. If the love of truth be pursued in artificial abstraction from the other claims which life makes on us, it is likely to degenerate into the love of error. God in His own indivisible nature is the only reality that must be sought and loved for its own sake alone.

Some men say, 'Religion consists in the docile and unintelligent acceptance of a mass of antiquated dogmas', and having said that, they think they have disposed of God. But let us not deceive ourselves. To say anything like that is to be guilty of a serious evasion. God does not want any man to accept, or pretend to accept, what he cannot believe. God's demand on me is not that I should force myself to accept a creed, nor is it by my acceptance or non-acceptance of any creed that I shall be judged by Him. Compelling oneself to believe is no part of true religion, even when the beliefs to which one tries to compel oneself *are* a part of it. It is truth itself that must do the compelling, not I. Faith is a gift of God; we cannot give it to ourselves. We cannot truly believe, and we ought not to try to make ourselves believe, unless that which we believe reveals itself to us as true. What God directly demands of us is therefore not belief, but 'truth in the inward parts'. Nothing could be more remote from the New Testament conception of faith than the schoolboy's definition of it (it was of course a very grown-up schoolboy who actually framed the definition) as 'believing what you know ain't true'. Let us not deceive ourselves by saying that Christ wants us to give up the quest for truth and accept Him instead. It is as the truth that He wants to be accepted, or not at all. 'Jesus saith unto him, I am ... the Truth.'[1]

There is here not only rebuke for dishonest evasion but also real comfort for honest perplexity. For if only we are honest in our quest, then what we find is not our responsibility but His whom we seek. Few things are so important in the spiritual life as to be able to distinguish God's burden from our own.

1. John 14: 6.

We can indeed never have the satisfaction of feeling that we are absolutely honest in our quest, for absolute honesty is something to which we mortals do not attain. Nevertheless we can distinguish less honest from more honest seeking, and there are some who are perplexed by the feeling that when they are seeking most honestly they are least able to find God. When they allow themselves to be carried 'whither the argument leads them', they find themselves being carried towards unbelief. That indeed is the very essence of intellectual doubt, and few Christians who have enjoyed a modern education can be complete strangers to the characteristic mental distress which it occasions. Nothing, however, could be more disastrous than that the pressure of this distress should be allowed to corrupt the probity of our thinking. God desires us both to think honestly and to believe, and unbelief and dishonest thinking are both involved in sin: but 'some sins ... are more heinous in the sight of God than others',[1] and without doubt dishonest belief is in His eyes a far more heinous thing than honest unbelief. To the perplexed seeker whose most diligent seeking for truth has seemed to lead him away from God and Christ it must therefore be said, 'Do not stop seeking, but look still deeper. Do not stop thinking, but think harder. Do not be less honest with yourself, but more honest.' My own testimony would have to be that in the long run nothing but harm has come to my faith from the many occasions on which I have yielded to the temptation of foreclosing my inquiries because they seemed to be leading me away from the faith rather than towards it. Whenever I have deliberately half-closed my eyes, for fear of seeing something inconvenient, I have always had to go back over that part of the road and walk it again with eyes as wide open as I could force them. For whatever it is that we are able to find by deliberately closing our eyes to what we fear to find, it is not God. It is an idol of our own imagining and not the true God. The true God is

1. *Westminster Shorter Catechism*, Q. 83.

rather He who will be found by us when, through keeping our eyes valiantly open to all that we now see, it is thereby given us to see yet more. He is not to be found aside from the realities of life, but as a yet deeper Reality behind them all. 'Let us delight', wrote St Augustine in his *Confessions*, 'to find Thee by failing to find Thee rather than by finding Thee to fail to find Thee.'[1]

To the spiritual perplexity which exercised so many of the rarest souls of the nineteenth century God appeared as a Being whom men desired to find but could not. But such a formula, though it truly represented one side of their situation, can never represent the whole of any human situation. For God is also a Being whom it ill suits any of us to find but from whom we cannot escape. Part of the reason why men cannot find God is that there is that in Him which they do not desire to find, so that the God whom they are seeking and cannot find is not the God who truly is. Perhaps we could not fail to find God, if it were really God whom we were seeking. And indeed the deepest reality of the situation is that contained in the discovery, which alone is likely at last to resolve our perplexity, that when we were so distressfully seeking that which was not really God, the true God had already found us, though at first we did not know that it was He by whom we had been found. There is a saying, 'Be careful what you seek; you might find it.' And some who have sought God only as a complacent ally of their own ambitions have found Him a consuming fire.

One of my colleagues in the scientific faculty of the University in which I now teach said to me recently, 'The difference between us men of science and you men of religion is that we are realists whereas you are romantics.' It is unfortunately but too true that many Christians have allowed their faith to be corrupted by the false 'enthusiasm' and *Schwärmerei* of an incurably romantic epoch, though I am sure that at least as many scientists have allowed their science to be so corrupted. But who could possibly read the Bible and call it a romantic literature? Rather it is devastating in its realism. There has never been a convert to Christianity who did not feel that in his conversion he was *facing up to the reality of things for the first time*, all his elaborate pretences having at last been broken down by the austere constraint of truth.

Where such a coercive factor is not present in the situation, there is indeed no true faith. God is not really found until we find not merely One whom we have long sought and could not find, but One who has all the time been seeking us and whom we have all the time been attempting to elude. If we seek God and think we cannot find Him, the question we should put to ourselves is whether, even as we seek, there is not One who is seeking us and whose solemn demands we are attempting to evade. Then the quest for God is like to turn into a quest for that in us which prevents our being found by Him. And with that we have drawn much nearer to the reality of the human situation. No man really believes so long as he can help believing. True belief is always belief that is under *the constraint of the Object* – which is therefore rather the Subject. And if today I can say that I believe, it is not at all that the so-called 'Will to Believe' has induced the belief, but that that which I believe has itself compelled my belief and because He in whom I believe has Himself wrought His own work in me. It no longer seems to me that it is I who am diligently wooing the divine Lover, but rather that, do what I will, the divine Lover will not let me be. It is not Truth that is coy, but I who am too faint-hearted to embrace it, lacking the courage to yield myself as I ought to its most inconveniently disturbing claims. It is not that by some great effort I am able to attain to belief, but that by no effort however great am I able to avoid it.

4

Thinking and Believing

THE rationalistic criticism of Christianity has recently found itself confronted with a very remarkable situation which seems to be causing it not a little salutary searching of heart. It had for long been accustomed to regard itself as alone representing the pure love of truth in the midst of a Christian world which played fast and loose with truth in the interest of its own prejudged fancies, whereas today it looks abroad upon a de-Christianized world where truth is increasingly flouted and where itself can find no more likely, or more valiant, ally than just the Christian Church.

It is worth while noticing how this changed situation has come about. During the long period of the Middle Ages there was no opposition between rationalism and Christianity. There was indeed one school of rationalists who opposed Christianity, namely, the Averroists, but it may fairly be said that they were beaten by the Christian philosophers on their own ground and at their own game. With that one exception the rationalists and the theologians were the self-same men. In the Middle Ages the greatest champions of reason were monks and priests. Those were days in which, when men forced their minds as wide open as they could get them, they found themselves constrained to a religious outlook. Those were days when the pure love of truth led men to believe in God.

But with the movement of thought known as the Renaissance there began to appear a number of thinkers of whom this was no longer true, and ever since then, down to our own time, the number of such thinkers has increased. During this modern period certain new currents of thought have played upon men's minds, with the result that when they have tried to think clearly, allowing themselves to be carried 'whither the argument led them', they have often found themselves, as the men of the Middle Ages did not find themselves, led away from the Christian faith. The intellectual presuppositions of the period, constituting as they did the outlook known as humanism, have indeed been such that this could hardly fail to be the case; and where these presuppositions have been accepted without question, and especially where their presence in the mind and influence on the argument have been so unconscious as to render them unavailable for criticism, those who shared them have been bound to regard Christian believers as deliberately shutting their eyes to the light. They honestly think of themselves as realists and of Christians as romantic illusionists. They honestly think of their own minds as being under the constraint of truth and of Christians as taking refuge in a world of dreams. They think they are facing a reality which Christians are afraid to face. They think they are sweetly reasonable while Christians are but the obscurantist defenders of a lost cause.

However, as I have just said, a remarkable change has now begun to overtake the situation. Rationalism, in thus freely following out its own destiny, has seemed to overreach itself, and in overreaching itself to turn back upon itself and pass into something very like its own opposite. We seem now, as M. Berdyaev said in that almost classic essay of his, to be at 'the End of the Renaissance'. 'The Renaissance', he wrote, 'began with the affirmation of man's creative individuality; it ended with its denial.'[1] And the thinning ranks of those who are still faithful to the old ideals of humanistic rationalism are now rubbing their eyes in the forlorn attempt to understand the fate that has overtaken their creed. I have known several such, and they are honest men lost in a pathetic bewilderment for which one can have only the deepest sympathy and understanding. As has been said by M. Jacques Maritain, who him-

1. *The End of our Time* (1919–23), English Translation (1933), p. 54.

self found his way back from such an outlook to the Christian faith, 'Rationalism, as it awaits the result of this promising growth, taking no account of its own responsibility, laments that the youth of the entire world should show at the moment such a lively appetite for collective forms and spiritual standardization, in despair of the unity which is lost.'[1] For indeed the old guard of humanistic rationalism is not only rubbing its eyes in bewilderment but also wringing its hands in despair, as it observes all its old watchwords being shouted down and its banners rudely spat upon – its freedom of thought and of speech and of assembly, its *liberté, égalité, fraternité*, its hard-won toleration, its rights of the individual, its liberalism, its democracy. But above all it wrings its hands in despair as it sees its cherished reason overborne by a deliberate and cynical irrationalism and its brave banner of truth dragged contemptuously in the dust by those who would raise up in its stead the garish banners of propaganda and the politic lie.

Where then is rationalism to look for any help in fighting its apparently losing battle against these new and powerful forces of unreason? I have already hinted at the answer. There are those within its ranks who are beginning to ask themselves whether their likeliest and most valiant ally may not strangely turn out to be their old enemy, the Christian Church. Who was it in Hitler's Germany that made the most effective stand for *liberté, égalité, fraternité*? Who was it that proved the most troublesome thorn in the side of the oppressors? Was it not the Christian Church, Roman and Protestant? Was it not a Christian pastor lying in prison and those who rallied round him beneath the banner of the Cross? Was it the anti-Christian forces that were now leagued on the side of honest thinking and open discussion and the pure love of truth, and the Christian forces that were leagued against these things? And is

1. *True Humanism* (English Translation of *L'humanisme intégral*, 1936), 1938, p. 153 f. The words 'promising growth' are of course charged with bitter irony.

it thus in Italy today,[1] in Japan, and in Russia, and in some quarters nearer home? Which are now the realists and which the illusionists? Does it not now look as if in the triumph of Christian principles lay the sole hope of survival for *any* of the ideals which the Renaissance held dear? Mayhap the time is coming, and even now is, when, instead of rationalistic dissent defending reasonableness and liberty and tolerance and democracy and the rights of the individual and a free science and learning and press against an unwilling or hesitating Church, the Church itself will be doing its lonely best to rescue the tattered remains of these standards from the non-Christian forces that are engaged in tearing them to pieces. Or if it be too much to say that the Church *as such* can engage itself in this struggle, at least it looks as if the most devoted members of the Church will be found standing in the foremost rank, and that they will have found their way there under pressure of their very Christian principles. I have recently heard many who do not themselves profess to be Christians – some of them Jews, and others without a conscious foothold in any faith but nevertheless cherishing the highest moral ideals – speak with eager hope of the leadership the Christian Church had it in its power to provide, and of their own readiness to make common cause with it against the new and deadly foe. Once again, then, as in the Middle Ages, reason and faith may be found fighting on the same side. Such a forecast will not, I trust, be misunderstood. It as little means that the spirit of the Renaissance must give way utterly before a new medievalism as that the faith of the Middle Ages must give way before a triumphant humanism. It means rather that Christianity must take up into itself what is true and well-founded in the humanistic protest, while humanism, abjuring the wild excesses and denials in which it has so often lost itself, must find its way back to the ultimate shelter of a full Christian commitment. In such an outlook the pure love of truth and the

1. 1942.

pure love of Christ will once again be able to join cordial hands and 'make one music as before'. And my point is that many lovers of truth who in former generations might have ranked themselves as critics and opponents of Christianity must *already* be beginning to ask themselves whether, as the lines are now drawn, their real place is not within – or very near – the Christian camp rather than in the ranks of Antichrist.

5

The By-way of Unreason

IT has been said that rationalism and humanism have at last so far overreached themselves that they are now passing into their own opposites. But the rationalism and humanism which have been overtaken by this fate were an essentially *man-centred* rationalism and humanism. The rationalism of the Ages of Faith was not man-centred but God-centred. And there is likewise a humanism which is God-centred rather than man-centred; that is, there is an outlook that allows full play for all those varied interests of human life to which Europe was reawakened by the Renaissance, and yet never forgets what the Ages of Faith so well knew – that man's chief end is to glorify God and to enjoy Him for ever. It is in the detachment of reason and humanity from this ultimate dependence upon the divine that the Christian is bound to seek the causes of their present eclipse. Man, when cut off from God, has relapsed into unreason. It is not unnatural, therefore, that many Christians should rejoice in the fate which has overtaken the Renaissance, as leading them back at last to the realities of the situation.

It is not unnatural that they should welcome the eclipse of the old detached rationalism by the new irrationalism, the eclipse of the old free-thought by the new authoritarianism, of the old individualism by the new collectivism, and even of the old liberalism by the new totalitarianism. And indeed we must be prepared to ask ourselves very seriously whether there is not behind these new movements and tendencies (if not exactly *in* them) something of a healthy revolt against the spirit that had previously dominated the modern world, and some elements of truth which must be given their rightful place in any future ordering of society.

Nevertheless I am convinced that some of the Christian thinkers of our time have allowed themselves to be too much caught in the current of the present reaction. Just as the theology of the eighteenth century tended to be too much affected by the rationalism then current, and the theology of the nineteenth by the characteristic contemporary blend of rationalism and romanticism, so the theology of our twentieth century tends to be too much affected by the current distrust and denial of reason. It is obviously no accident that the appearance of certain extreme anti-liberal movements in theology has closely synchronized with the appearance of the extreme anti-liberal movements in politics. The two are plainly parallel products of the same spirit of the age. Hitler himself understands this very well. 'The greatness of every powerful organization which embodies a creative idea', he writes, 'lies in the spirit of religious devotion and intolerance with which it stands out against all others, because it has an ardent faith in its own right. If an idea is right in itself and, furnished with the fighting weapons I have mentioned, wages war on this earth, then it is invincible, and persecution will only add to its internal strength. The greatness of Christianity did not arise from attempts to make compromises with those philosophical opinions of the ancient world which had some resemblance to its own doctrine, but from the unrelenting and fanatical proclamation and defence of its own teaching.'[1] The fact that the two movements are often found opposing each other, and that the most valiant stand against the neo-pagan authoritarianisms has sometimes been made from the point of view of an extreme Christian authoritarianism, need not surprise us. Just in the same fashion did the Christian apologists of the eighteenth century, like Butler and Conybeare and Sherlock and Paley, most valiantly oppose the deistic attack upon Christianity, though standing upon the self-same typically eighteenth-

1. *Mein Kampf*, translated by James Murphy, London (1939), Vol. I, Chapter XII, p. 294.

century platform – so that today we are almost more struck by the resemblance between the outlooks of the deists and the apologists than by the difference between them. In that day the abstract rationalism of unbelief was met by an equally abstract Christian rationalism; in our day the new unbelieving authoritarianisms are met by an equally uncompromising Christian authoritarianism. Previously reason was met by reason, whereas now unreason is met by unreason. I am myself convinced that the new situation is as unsatisfactory as was the old. I am convinced that the right way to have tackled the eighteenth-century opposition would have been to challenge its conception of reason, and that the right way to tackle the new opposition is to challenge its irrational authoritarianism. The method so many of our new counsellors are advising us to follow is to confront anti-Christian dogmatism with Christian dogmatism, an unreasonable paganism with an equally unreasonable Christianity. Some of these counsellors would even seek to win recognition for the superiority of Christianity by attempting to show that it is *more* unreasonable than any paganism. It is only, they say, when thought is put completely out of court that faith can emerge. Much of this advice is given under the influence of the writings of Sören Kierkegaard, the long-neglected Danish thinker from whom the thought of our time might learn so many salutary and badly-needed lessons, if only it could do so without allowing itself to be carried away by his many intemperate prejudices. Of Kierkegaard's conception of the nature of Christian faith my own old teacher, the late Professor Hugh Mackintosh, has written thus: 'Faith on these terms is blind defiance. The way into the Kingdom lies through the simple crucifixion of intelligence. Reason is stunned – rendered unconscious, as it were – by the logical enormities thrust upon it by the Gospel.'[1] Those who follow this teaching take as their particular charter St Paul's language in the early chapters of his first letter to the Corinthians, when

1. *Types of Modern Theology* (1937), p. 247.

he says that after 'the world by wisdom knew not God, it pleased God by the foolishness of preaching to save them that believe', that 'God hath chosen the foolish things of the world to confound the wise', and that 'the wisdom of this world is foolishness with God'.[1] Corinth was a Greek city given over to the profitless logomachies of the philosophical and theosophical schools of the late Hellenistic age, and it was simple fact that the new light of truth which St Paul had to offer appeared to its intelligentsia as foolishness when placed beside their own *gnosis* and *sophia*. We cannot doubt that the great Apostle was wisely guided in refusing to enter into argument with them and preferring a very different and more direct approach. 'Very well,' he says to them, 'my Gospel *is* foolishness if you will, but its foolishness is wiser than your wisdom.' St Paul's situation in respect to Corinth is one that has frequently been repeated in the history of the Christian Church. Especially has it often been repeated in those post-Renaissance centuries and societies, already referred to, in which the search for truth seemed to be leading men away from faith rather than towards it. Such, for instance, was John Wesley's situation in the rationalistic and deistic England of the eighteenth century, and his famous remark after visiting the new Octagon Unitarian Chapel at Norwich is very much in the same spirit as St Paul's language on receiving from the household of Chloe such disquieting information about the state of things in Corinth. 'How can it be thought', he said, 'that the old coarse Gospel should find admission here?'[2]

But of course Wesley very well knew that it was only to a false refinement that the Gospel appeared coarse, just as St Paul knew that it was only to a false wisdom that it appeared foolish. We must not be so humourless as to found a theological theory upon a misunderstanding of such language. For every once in the Bible when the Gospel is spoken of as foolish-

1. 1 Corinthians 1: 21, 27; 3: 19.
2. *Journal of John Wesley*, Everyman Library edition, Vol. II, p. 399.

ness in comparison with the wisdom of the Greek schools, there are ten times when it is spoken of as a higher wisdom, a sounder knowledge, and a more liberating truth. And in a day like our own, when the world is like to perish from the contempt of reason rather than from its too unremitting exercise, in a day when unreason and blind dogmatism and 'bluff' and 'propaganda' seem to have it all their own way, the Church must not hesitate to press this bolder claim. It must speak to men in the name of a truth the knowledge of which can alone make them free. It must counsel not the despair of thought but its harder and more honest exercise. Much as I have learned from many of the theologians of the Barthian school, the straitest sect of them both puzzle and distress me by the way they speak of what they call 'human reason'. They distress me because their language bears too suspicious a resemblance to the language of the totalitarian propagandists whom nevertheless many of them most staunchly and gallantly oppose. They puzzle me because I do not think I know what this 'human reason' is of which they so glibly speak. Reason is after all not something that we observe in men so much as something that we desiderate for them. It belongs, in Kantian language, not to the sphere of things *a posteriori*, but to the sphere of things *a priori*, which means that it belongs essentially to heaven rather than to earth. Logic is not the description of how men *actually* think – God help it if it were! – but of how they ought to think – and usually do not. It is the description of how God meant us to think, and hence is the reflected image of His own thought – the *Abbild*, as the Germans say, of which His thought is the *Urbild*. Dr L. P. Jacks once remarked that 'God is pleased when the publications of the Rationalist Press are really rational, and angry when they are not.' There could be no more salutary reminder. What is wrong with the world is not that it thinks but that it refuses to think. There is of course a situation in which 'the native hue of resolution is sicklied o'er by the pale cast of thought'; but such thinking is not good thinking. And what is wrong with the world is not that it reasons too well but that it does not reason well enough. That man is reasonable who looks things as they are straight in the face. It was to do this, and to do nothing else, that reason was given us. Reason may be defined as the ability to recognize truth when it is presented to us, and it is an ability which we show no great sign of possessing or at least of using. What should be spoken of depreciatingly is therefore not human reason but human unreasonableness, not human logic but human lack of logic. As Professor de Burgh has said, 'Only when, in our arrogance, we take the human mind as the measure, can we plausibly speak of God as superrational, or of our faith in his revelation as transcending the bounds of reason.'[1] Faith and reason must not then be enemies but the best of friends. 'Not all who believe think,' wrote St Augustine in his most characteristic manner, 'but he who thinks believes. He believes in thinking and thinks in believing.'

The theologians of whom I have spoken, and whom I regard as too much caught in the current of the contemporary wave of irrationalism, would have little sympathy with my present attempt to defend the reasonableness of the Christian faith. They would not indeed find it easy to speak at all 'in defence of the Christian religion'. They have abjured all apologetics and confine themselves to the practice of dogmatics. That is to say, they will announce to us the Christian message but will neither refute our unbelief nor tell us why we are to believe. In this change of front from the method of the old apologetics there is, as I believe, a certain important element of wisdom. In the past men have been offered all sorts of irrelevant reasons for believing; all sorts of extraneous considerations have been adduced in support of belief. The attempt was made to supply the Christian Gospel with a variety of flying buttresses no one of which was really essential to its

1. *From Morality to Religion*, p. 286.

stability, and some of which were far more shaky than any part of the edifice itself – so that, in collapsing, as they frequently did, they were not unlikely to pull down some adjacent part of the edifice along with them. But there is only one good reason for believing, and that is the perception of the inherent truth of the Gospel itself. What we must do, therefore, is to allow the Gospel to do its own work, and to carry its own conviction. In that sense I am in full sympathy with the present preference of the dogmatic approach to the older apologetic one, and I think I may say that I have always tried to follow it, however unsuccessfully. It is high time we Christian theologians stopped apologizing for Christ and took thought rather to confront men with His imperious claim. The great age of modern apologetics was the eighteenth century, and there is no literature that seems more dead today than the writings of those eighteenth-century defenders of the faith, unless indeed it be the deistic writings against which they were directed.

But we are *not* allowing the Gospel to do its own work unless we present it to the men of our time in the form in which the profound truth of it is most likely to be evident to them. If we present the Gospel in the form which brought most conviction to the men of the fourth century, or of the thirteenth or of the sixteenth, we are likely to be presenting it in a form which may actually obscure its relevance to the problems and trials of today. It is possible to state the Christian message in a way which, without actually falsifying its content, is almost certain to prevent its assimilation by the minds of those we are addressing. And on the other hand it is possible to substitute the dogmatic for the apologetic approach without being content merely to state the Christian message in its most abstract and timeless form (or even in the only too time-conditioned form given to it by a particular age in the past) and then inviting men to take it or leave it. Dogmatic theology should not be taught thus dogmatically. Dogmatic theology is the name of a good thing; but dogmatism is the name of a bad thing, and the sole reason why the bad thing which it is has come to be called by that name is that it has far too often been exemplified in the deliverances of the dogmatic theologians of the past. Being myself a dogmatic theologian by profession, I must at all costs avoid this error. I might say, therefore, that in what follows I shall be trying to present Christian dogma in a way that is not dogmatic. Yet it is not really dogma that I shall be presenting, but something more important, something prior to all dogma (that is, prior to all ecclesiastical definition, which is what dogma means), something out of which all true dogma, including such dogma as there is in the New Testament, originally emerged, namely, the personal dealings of the Christian soul with God. I shall be concerned with what St Bonaventure in the thirteenth century called the *itinerarium mentis in Deum*, or with what John Bunyan in the seventeenth called the Christian pilgrim's progress; though what I say may be in some ways as different from the Calvinistic puritanism of the one as from the Franciscan mysticism of the other. What I shall try to do, so far as is possible within so narrow a compass, is to show that the Christian of all men walks through this present world with eyes most widely open to the realities of the situation in which he is placed.

6

The Encounter

THE beginning of the itinerary, like all true beginnings, *abiit in mysterium*. It came in earliest childhood when, with the awakening of self-consciousness, we first learned the use of I and Thou; which is very good reason for its being hidden in mystery, since memory can go back no further than self-consciousness, it being obviously impossible to recall a state of mind of which we were not conscious at the time. In this first encounter of the *ego* with the *alter*, this first conflict of self-will with the will of another, self-consciousness was born. All my own earliest memories have in them such an element of encounter, of having to adjust my own nature and will to a nature and will not my own. I cannot remember a time when my life seemed to me to be my own to do with as I pleased. From the very beginning its centre was not itself or in me, but outside itself and me. I was of course, in the first instance, under the authority of the elder members of the household – so that in that as in other respects I was born a Presbyterian! I was under orders, and it was from my father or my mother or my nurse that the orders came. Yet my earliest memories clearly contain the knowledge that these elders did but transmit and administer an authority of which they were not themselves the ultimate source. For I never supposed that it was merely a case of my father's or mother's will being pitted against my will, still less of their power being pitted against my weakness. I knew they had a *right* to ask of me what they did and that I had no right to refuse what they asked; that is, I knew that what they desired of me was right and that my own contrary desire was wrong. But I knew also that their desiring it did not make it right, but that they desired it because it was already right independently of their desire. In other words, I understood that my parents were under the same constraint that they were so diligent in transmitting to me. Not, of course, that this constraint dictated the self-same actions and abstentions in them and in me. The little girl in *Punch*, who had justified her use of a certain unmaidenly expression by the plea that 'Daddy says it,' only to be told that Daddy was Daddy, is reported to have replied, 'Well, I'm I'm.' My own father did not allow himself the use of such expressions, yet I understood very well that much was allowable for him that was not allowable for me, and that still more was incumbent on him that was not incumbent on me. But I knew also that in all this he was no more pleasing himself than he was allowing me to please myself. Had he given me the impression that it was merely his good pleasure I was called upon to obey, had he exercised an authority under which he showed no sign of standing himself, had he expected of me a way of life which bore no relation to his own way of living, his influence and authority over me could have had little of the character which in fact I felt them to possess. Actually, the way he himself lived, and the kind of being he was, exercised over me a more powerful and lasting constraint than all his spoken words of command.

I have been saying that I knew all this, and I think I did know it. This does not mean that I could then have explicitly formed in my mind any such propositions as the above, still less that I could have found words in which to express them. I could not then have isolated, with a view to contemplating them separately, any of the pieces of knowledge of which I have now spoken. Yet I am quite sure that they were all implicitly present in my mind.

There came a day, indeed, when I was awakened to the limitations of my presbyterian system by the discovery that elders are not infallible. In my case it was not by any means a rude awakening, but it was something of a shock none the less. There came a day and an occasion when it seemed clear that my mother was wrong in asking a certain thing of me and that I had some real justification for withholding obedience. Yet it is important to notice that this day could never have come if I had begun by supposing that my mother herself was the source of the authority which was given her to administer. Nor was the new situation which had now emerged to be confused for a moment with a mere conflict of wills. That, unfortunately, would have been nothing new. What was new was the conflict of *judgements*; not that my parents wanted one thing of me while I wanted another thing for myself, but that my parents judged something to be *right* for me which I did not judge to be right for myself.

What then was the ultimate source of the authority which my parents were thus doing their fallible best to administer and under which they stood no less than I? What was this constraint that was laid on us? Whose was this greater will that we were both called upon to obey? Whom were my parents pleasing, since they were not pleasing themselves, and whom did they want me to please in pleasing them? Once again, I have no memory of a time when I did not know the answer. From the beginning I knew that it was God.

But there is something else that is in my earliest memories and to which I have so far made only a passing reference, namely, the presence in myself of a tendency to rebel against the constraint which was thus exercised over me. By this I do not mean at all the judgement, of which I have spoken as first emerging at a much later period, that my parents were not infallible in their understanding of this constraint and sometimes made mistakes in its application. I mean, on the contrary, that there was that in me which, without doubting the rightness of their judgement, nevertheless rebelled against it. My word for this was *naughtiness* and, as I say, the knowledge that there was such naughtiness in me is unmistakably present in my earliest memories. What then was this naughtiness? I have no hesitation in saying that its essence lay in the tendency to find the centre of my life in myself, to behave as though I were the centre of my world. Its essence was self-will, which of course does not mean that I had a will of my own – for I was always told that it was good to have a will of my own and that I had not nearly enough of one – but rather that I often used such will as I had to assert my independence of the Greater Will whose behests had been made known to me, though I knew I ought rather to make it the obedient servant of the Greater Will. I knew that when I was naughty I was taking the management of things into my own hands instead of allowing myself to be managed by God; and I knew that in so doing I was putting things badly out of joint. The word naughtiness means no-wight-i-ness. The naughty wight is therefore no true wight, no true man. And this too I understood. I knew that when I put self in the centre of things, I was putting myself where no man, not even a father, has any right to be. For I knew that at the real centre of things is only God.

Such then was for me the starting-point of the itinerary, and though I could not then have analysed it as I have analysed it now, I feel confident that my present analysis is in the main correct. All I have said will indeed strike some as being almost ridiculously familiar. Why then have I wearied them with it? It is because even at this early stage in the journey the most radical groups of dissentients will already have begun to leave our Christian company and follow another track. Some of these will say that I have wrongly analysed my memories. They will try to persuade me that I started from a human consciousness in which God was not yet. Some will contend that the tension between my own will and Another's was not really primitive but was a later development, while others will allow that it was primitive, but will contend that the other will in question was only the will of my parents or other elders. Still others there are, however, who without questioning the fidelity of my memories will say that the experiences I have described were the result of the particular way in which I was brought up.

With these last I must readily agree. I should indeed be an ingrate to do otherwise. I know well that if I had received no upbringing at all, I could not have had any of these experiences. I know also that had I been brought up by savages instead of by Christian parents, my experiences would have been very different from what in fact they were. Yet I believe that even then they would have borne a certain genealogical resemblance to the experiences I have described. All that we know of the mentality of savages goes to confirm this. We know of no human beings, however backward and barbarous, who do not seem to be under constraint to some system of what are called taboos; and taboos are never conceived as proceeding *merely* from the will of the elders, or from any human will, but always also from some super-human source. Yet I do not think it is on such empirical confirmation that I should rest my own belief in the essential universality of such experiences. It is rather that I have difficulty in conceiving any mentality which was already genuinely *human* and yet did not in some way conform to this fundamental pattern.

This analysis of my own infant experience I am fully prepared to defend with further argument, with the only kind of argument that could here be in question, namely, a still more detailed analysis of it. And I should be fully prepared to defend my further contention that the fundamental structure of this experience, as regards at least those aspects of it which I have so far mentioned, is common not only to those who like myself have been brought up in the Christian tradition but also to those brought up in any of the earlier traditions of our race. Every tradition is governed by a constraint which is, as we say, at the same time moral and religious. Every tradition is the *traditio* of a *mos* which is associated with a *numen*. But I am more concerned to take issue with a group of dissentients who would agree to all this and would nevertheless part company with us at this same early stage in our progress. They would agree that all traditional human experience has been as we have described it, but they would hold that in these latter days there has emerged a possible type of human experience which differs radically from it.

Some of these would say that whereas the race has up till now lived under such a constraint as I have described, they themselves are aware of living under no such constraint. They have no scruples, moral or religious. They see no reason why they should not dispose their lives round a centre interior to themselves or why they should not be, in the poet's phrase, captains of their own souls. One such writer of a widely-read book of popular philosophy recently made himself responsible for the declaration, 'I have no conscience, so far as I can discover. I am a stranger to all the traditional experiences of moral conflict and the struggle against temptation.' What did he mean? We do sometimes say of certain people that they have no conscience, meaning either that they do certain dreadful things without any apparent awareness that they should not do them or (more commonly perhaps) that, though they do possess this awareness, they do not allow it to exercise any restraining influence on the doing of them. Did the popular philosopher mean that he was one of these? And did he mean that, being tempted to do all sorts of wrong things, he never struggled against such temptation but gave way to it at once? If he did, then he is indeed a dangerous fellow whom all prudent men, and not least his own kind, will be anxious to avoid. Or did he mean rather that he never *was* so tempted and that he was therefore able to fulfil all righteousness – for instance, to do always unto others as he would have others do unto him – without any struggle at all? When he said that he had no conscience, did he mean that he had no sense of actual or possible discrepancy between duty and inclination, his inclinations being always of the noblest and purest and most unselfish kind? In that case I should like to know what his wife has to say in the matter, and what others who are his daily associates have to say. I do not know of any *third* meaning that can be attached to the popular philosopher's protestation. It means either that he is aware of no obligation to think of others as well as of himself or that he has no natural tendency to consult his own interest to the neglect of others. Well, all I can say is that neither of these things is true of me. Whatever else of my childhood's outlook I have put behind me, I have never been able to put this behind me. My life has never been free from this conflict and tension. I have always known that certain rightful demands were being made upon me and that I was not properly responding to these demands. If this counts as part of Christian belief, then I must confess that I have never had any difficulty in believing this part of Christianity: my difficulty has always lain rather in any attempt to escape its too obvious truth.

The more common way of dissent has, however, been to admit the continuance of the conflict but to deny the traditional interpretation of it. There certainly runs through all our life a tension between two opposing entities, but – so it is now said – these two entities are not, as used to be supposed, the divine Will and the human will, but something quite different and much less mysterious. What then are they? The humanistic thought of the last three centuries has been immensely fertile of suggested answers to this question. Indeed, one cannot altogether withhold admiration as one contemplates the amazing ingenuity that has been called into play in order to escape the Christian reading of the situation. Even from so short a book as Henry Sidgwick's *Outlines of the History of Ethics* one can gain some idea of the variety of expedients to which resort has been had in the attempt to keep hold of morals while letting God go. And yet I think that all the proposals may without injustice be reduced to three simple types.

First, there are those who attempt to show that the two conflicting entities, instead of being God and man, are only two different parts of man's own self. The duality is there, but it is a duality within human nature. We are indeed aware of a demand, but it is a demand made by the higher upon the lower self. The tension is a tension between two desires, both equally natural; and in no sense a tension between the natural and the supernatural. Now there was a time in my undergraduate days as a student of philosophy when I was almost tempted to believe that some such explanation could be consistently carried through. But I very soon came to see that all such explanations are based on sophisms. For it became quite clear to me that the tension in question was never merely between two parts of my *existing* nature, but between my actual and my ideal nature. Of the two parts of my nature that are here said to be in conflict one does not exist; it only ought to exist. The tension is never merely between two desires, but essentially between the desir*ed* and the desir*able*, that is, between what I actually do desire and what I know I ought to desire but for the most part do not. And again, it is a plain sophism to say that the conflict is between my lower and my higher self, unless you go on at once to explain to me what is meant by calling one self 'higher' than the other and why, if I actually possess both selves, an obligation should be laid on me to prefer the one to the other. Obviously the real tension is not between a higher and a lower self, but between my clear knowledge that I am called upon to prefer the one self and my strong actual tendency to give preference to the other. Nothing seems clearer to me now than that the conflict which I experience cannot possibly be regarded as merely interior to myself, but can only be caused in me by a constraint coming to me from beyond myself.

Second, there are those who would admit this, but would persuade me that the constraint does not come to me from God but only from *other men*, that is, from the society of which I am a member. The conflict I experience is a conflict between my own private will and the will of society at large. It is this society which claims me and is the source of the obligation which I feel. Now if the contention had been that the conflict was between my own desire and the *good* of the society, I should have had to agree that such was often the case. But the good of society does not mean what society is but what it ought to be; nor (unfortunately) does it mean what society wills but what it ought to will and usually does not; not therefore what it desires but what it *owes* – for 'ought' and 'owes' are originally parts of the same verb. And if it be asked *to whom* society owes this duty, I am sure the answer can only be that it owes it to God. But not for a moment will I listen to the suggestion that the obligation of which I am aware comes from the *will* of the society. Good democrat though I am, I am aware of no obligation to subject my will to the will of society. Rather am I aware of an obligation, laid upon society corporately as much as upon myself individually, to subject our wills to a higher will than either of us can boast of possessing, and to conform to a higher standard than either of us can boast of exemplifying. If society were the source of obligation, then society could not itself be obliged to be one thing rather than another. But I know well that society is so obliged. It cannot therefore be itself the *fons et origo* of the claim which it rightfully makes upon me. And all this I knew in my own way in my childhood, just as I knew that my father and mother were not themselves the ultimate sources of the claim which they exercised over me.[1]

But thirdly and finally, there are other and subtler arguers who would allow me all this, who would admit that the obligation I feel cannot be explained merely in terms of my own

1. 'The fact that man brings something to his social relations and is not completely a product of them, is, of course, the ground both of his power to act anti-socially and of his power to act responsibly as a member of the social whole.... It is the conviction that man has a status in the universe otherwise than through his place in the social order that is the reason for belief in democracy and also for the problems of that political faith. For it means that the human being, far from being free in himself and only under authority in his social relationships, is in fact within the sphere of authority in himself by virtue of his relation to the supertemporal order, and therefore enters his temporal relations responsibly.' – V. A. Demant, *The Religious Prospect* (1939), p. 33 f.

psychology, nor of the psychology of society, but must flow from a source more ultimate than either, yet who would have me believe that this source is something much less than what we mean by the word God. What then is this reality which is more than man but less than God? It has been given various names according to the changing fashions of different philosophical generations – it has been spoken of as the eternal moral law or the eternal moral order, as a spiritual principle, as a realm of values. These names make it clear that it differs from what we mean by God in being abstract and impersonal, whereas God is personal and concrete. The upholders of this view often rely for its defence on the ancient philosophical distinction between two kinds of being, essence and existence, and their contention is that the moral order or realm of values, whose sovereign authority over me I am fain to acknowledge, is not something that exists but only 'a realm of essences'. This type of philosophy always reminds me of the schoolboy who defined an abstract noun as 'the name of something which does not exist, like honour or truthfulness'. The distinction between essence and existence is a most necessary and valuable one, as was well understood both in ancient Greece and in the Middle Ages, but it is a distinction, not between two separate ways in which something may be, but between two aspects of the being of whatever has being. A law, an order, a principle, a value – these can have no being of any sort when taken by themselves. Taken by themselves they are merely abstractions which our minds make, for their own purposes, from the concrete reality in which they inhere and by which our minds are confronted. There cannot therefore be a realm of trans-human values which has essence but no existence, or which subsists in isolation in a merely general form. The universal and the particular are not two different kinds of reality but two elements in the reality of all that is real. And as for the attempt to persuade me that the reality which constrains me is an *impersonal* reality, I can only reply that such a notion is plainly ruled out by the nature of the constraint itself. Impersonal realities do indeed exercise over me some kinds of constraint, as does the wind when it constrains me to battle against it or the rain when it compels me to take shelter. But the constraint of which I have been speaking is of a wholly different kind; it is a constraint to be pure-minded and loyal-hearted, to be kind and true and tender, and to love my neighbour as myself. And what could possibly be meant by saying that any reality of an impersonal kind could exercise over me such a constraint as that? I have never been able to see that it could mean anything at all. I have never been able to see how any being that is not a person could possess a moral and spiritual claim over me. That is why, as Dr Emil Brunner says, 'it is so much more comfortable to have a pantheistic philosophy than to believe in a Lord God.... A God who is neuter makes no claims; He simply allows Himself to be looked at.'[1]

I take it as certain, therefore, that the moral and spiritual life of man can have no real meaning apart from God. It is out of man's dealings with God that this moral and spiritual life has emerged and, if God is made to disappear from it, nothing at all of it is left – nothing, that is, that is characteristically human. 'I have never', said Dostoyevsky, 'been able to conceive mankind without Him.' This does not mean that men may not continue to feel themselves under a certain moral constraint even after they have adopted an atheistic philosophy. A railway engine does not stop as soon as the driver shuts off the steam, nor does a turnip wither and die as soon as it is pulled out of mother earth. Within the modern humanistic era there have been many shining examples of men who had given up all belief in God and were nevertheless filled with a zeal for righteousness, and a love of neighbour, which might put many Christians to shame. There has even been seen in the world such a thing as a professed and professional atheist manifesting

1. *Man in Revolt* (English translation of *Der Mensch in Widerspruch*), p. 432.

in his own deeds the fruit of Christian love. But it would appear that this is likely to be no more than a very temporary phenomenon. It cannot last long, and it may be that it has already largely passed away.[1] The nineteenth-century opponents of Christian belief largely shared the Christian estimate of moral values. They may not have believed in God, but they did believe in justice and in mercy, in honour and in truth, in the rights of the weak, and in the existence in all men of a spiritual birthright which had preference over all differences of race and colour and blood and nation. But of the present-day opposition to Christianity this has already ceased to be true. It looks as if the Christian moral standards were now sharing the fate of the Christian idea of God. Naturally this causes almost as much pain to those who still share the outlook of nineteenth-century unbelief as to Christian believers themselves; they are appalled as they look out upon the contemporary scene. What they do not understand is their own responsibility in the matter. What they do not understand is the strictly inevitable nature of this distressing and disastrous result; or, as has been said by Miss Rosalind Murray in that remarkable book of hers, *The Good Pagan's Failure*, the modern 'good pagan' does not understand that 'such development was intrinsic in his outlook, though he himself did not envisage it.'[2] He 'demanded the impossible when he pushed the cart over the hill, and over the brow, and told it to stop half-way down.'[3] This is the conclusion towards which I have

---

1. 'Appreciation of the humanitarian Christian virtues is like the enjoyment of the fruits which have been cut off from the living tree. Cut freshly, these fruits are still infused with something of the original life from which they came. Preserved through time on the ice of habit, discipline, moral education, they may keep some of their flavour, though icy. But sooner or later – and sooner rather than later – the fruit grows woody and withers, and we have to return to the living tree for more. (This is our state today.)' – Louis Arnaud Reid, *Preface to Faith* (1939), p. 181 f.

2. p. 56.   3. *Ibid.*

been moving in all that I have said so far. My argument has been that if God be subtracted from the total spiritual situation which my earliest memories disclose and in which I have ever since continued to stand, *nothing at all of it is left*. I stand now, as I stood then, under the sovereign constraint of One who has never ceased to make it known to me that He claimed me for His own and required me for His service. It is clear then that for my own part I have no choice but to set my feet upon the pilgrim's way.

7

The Challenge and the Promise

SPURGEON, the great preacher, had a story about one of his fellow ministers who went to the house of a poor old woman with a contribution of money for the payment of her rent. He knocked again and again, but failed to get any response. Nevertheless the old woman was all the time within, and her explanation afterwards was, 'I heard the knocking, but I thought it was the man come to ask for the rent.'

That is a perfect parable of the next great misunderstanding to which we must turn our attention. I have already argued that at the foundation of the whole spiritual life of man there lies the knowledge of a transcendent claim that is made upon him. We have all heard this knocking at the door. We have been hearing it all our lives through. We hear it now, in this present moment. It stirs us at the very core of our being, and somewhere deep down in our hearts we all have some understanding of what it means. But what we understand in the bottom of our hearts we often sadly misunderstand with 'the top of our minds'.

He who stands at the door has come with a gift, but we are so ready to think that He has come for a payment. The knock is a Saviour's knock, but we are so ready to think it a Taskmaster's. That is perhaps the greatest misunderstanding to which religion has been subject in every age. It is the common error of most pre-Christian and non-Christian forms of religion, and it is also the error which has done most to falsify and limit the true understanding of Christianity itself. We interpret the divine summons merely as a demand for obedient service, and so we try to still the knocking by feverish action.

We turn our religion into a code of good conduct, an ideal to be striven for, a law to be obeyed.

All these have indeed their own part to play within the Christian life. Law and commandment, good conduct and the quest of the ideal, hard work and loyal service must all be given due place; and to deny them place would be to fall into the error opposite to that which we are now considering. But their place is not at the root of the spiritual life. They are not of the root but of the fruit.

Christianity is, when fundamentally regarded, not a law but a gospel. It was as a gospel that it was preached from the very beginning. The word 'gospel' or (in its original Greek form) 'evangel' means good news; and good news is precisely what Christianity sets out to be. The little wireless listener who, on being taken to church for the first time, remarked that she 'liked the music better than the news', well understood what the sermon was meant to be, however just or unjust may have been her estimate of its quality on that occasion. The Gospel is news of salvation. It is news of redemption. It is news, not of rent demanded, but of rent paid.

This, however, is not to say that the Gospel does not make its own demands on us, though they are demands very different from the demands of mere law. Something is expected of the man who hears good news, no less than of the man who is merely reminded of his debts and duties, though it is not the same thing that is expected. Something was expected of the old woman in the parable – and she tragically failed to fulfil the expectation. She was expected to open the door. There was no summons to give but there was a summons to receive.

I have already testified to my awareness of a transcendent constraint under which I have at all times stood, a transcendent demand which has been made upon me from my youth up. When, however, I reflect further on this demand, I see clearly that it is not so much a demand that I should do something as a demand that I should allow something be done in me. It is not that I am expected to produce something out of myself, or to achieve something in my own strength, but that I am expected to allow Another to work His will with me. The demand is much more fundamentally a demand for surrender than a demand for effort. I am asked, not to assert my will, but to yield it; or rather I *am* asked to assert it, but only that I may will its surrender. 'Our wills', the poet says, 'are ours to make them Thine.' Here again is something which I always somehow understood, though I could not at first have analysed it in this reflective way. I always knew that this constraint was being laid upon me for my own good and that in yielding to it lay my final happiness. And I knew also that what was wanted of me to this end was only that I should allow myself to be *taken in charge*.

At the root of all human spirituality there lies some understanding of this fact, but it is only in Christianity that the fullness of its meaning has been revealed. The essence of the Christian Gospel is that the demands of the law under which we were held have already been fulfilled for us by Him whose the law is. The righteousness which is demanded of us, and which we are unable to achieve, has been achieved for us and is now freely offered to us. God Himself, in the person of Christ the Son, has satisfied His own claims upon us. When Christ died on Calvary, the sacrifice we could not offer was offered for us, the debt we could not pay was paid for us – both figures have had large place in the history of Christian thought. The Christian good news is that all that is demanded of us has already been accomplished for us – was for ever accomplished when Jesus Christ, as He died, said 'It is finished.' Our salvation is already secured. It is there for us to take. We must not try to win it; all we need do is to receive it. Or again, as the New Testament so often expresses it, all we need do is to *believe* it – to believe that it has already been won. Salvation, we are told, is not by works but by faith. Christ Himself said,

'All things are possible to him that believeth.'[1] And St Paul said, 'For Christ is the end of the law to everyone that believeth.'[2] 'And by him all that believe are justified from all things, from which ye could not be justified by the law of Moses.'[3] 'The gospel of Christ ... is the power of God unto salvation to every one that believeth.'[4] But the two ways of stating the matter are really equivalent. Readiness to receive is the same as readiness to believe. To believe that all has already been done for us is to be willing to take it all as a free gift, instead of trying either to achieve it for ourselves or to deserve it as a reward of achievement.

The Gospel, that last text said, is *power*. That is what it is here so necessary to understand. It is what all moralistic misreadings of Christianity completely fail to understand. 'Mony an hungry, starving creature', said the blind Covenanter woman to Morton in Scott's *Old Mortality*, 'when he sits down on a Sunday forenoon to get something that might warm him to his great work, has a dry clatter o' morality driven about his lugs.'[5] But Christ did not come to earth to tell us merely what we ought to do; He came to do something for us. He came not merely to exhort but to help. He did not come to give us good advice. That, if it were no more than that, was possibly not a thing of which we stood greatly in need, for there are always plenty of people who are ready with their advice. Advice is cheap, but what Christ offered us was infinitely costly. It was the power of God unto salvation.

Christianity thus differs from all mere ethical systems in that it reveals to us not merely the nature of the ideal but the nature of the real. It reveals not merely what ought to be but what is. It tells not of something to be accomplished but of something already accomplished. It is not a programme of 'moral rearmament'; it is news about reality. The New Testament does not

1. Mark 9 : 23.   2. Romans 10 : 4.
3. Acts 13 : 39.   4. Romans 1 : 16.
5. Chapter xlii.

say, 'Ye shall know the rules, and by them ye shall be bound', but 'Ye shall know the truth, and the truth shall make you free.'[1] Hence its fundamental proclamation (its *kerygma*, as it is in the Greek) is set not in the imperative but in the indicative. The aorist indicative is indeed the New Testament's favourite tense. 'God so *loved* the world that he *gave* ...'[2] It is a tense that speaks of an action completed, of something that was done once, and once for all. Here alone resides the power of the Christian message. It is small wonder, then, that those versions of Christianity which have reduced it to a mere programme of human action, and not least those versions which have reduced it to a *social* programme, should so sadly fail in their appeal and find themselves threatened with ignominious defeat at the hands of anti-Christian movements which have precisely this advantage over them – that they have at least the character of a religion in offering men a faith (even if a false one) as well as a programme and as the basis of a programme. This has been so admirably stated by Mr V. A. Demant in his book on *The Religious Prospect* that I shall take leave to quote some sentences of his instead of trying to say the same thing in my own words. 'In the period of rationalistic Liberalism ... man's relatedness to the larger reality was proclaimed as a moral ideal rather than as an essential fact. It was offered for the direction of his purposes; it was not affirmed as the ground of his existence. He was taught that he was an individual, but that he ought to realize his relatedness. He was nagged into becoming a good social being of a cooperative atom in the spiritual world. The whole experiment was a valiant attempt at works without faith. The totalitarian revolt discloses the need and the ground of the faith that had been lost, the faith that man is essentially a being in relation to a super-individual whole. This relatedness is not only the object but the root of his being. Totalitarian philosophies proclaim to men that their individual lives derive significance from a larger

1. John 8: 32.   2. John 3: 16.

and stronger life which upholds them, carries them over individual and temporary failure, and assures them of personal fulfilment on condition of complete surrender. The formal resemblance of this assurance to that offered by religious faith makes totalitarianism a force which colours the whole religious situation.... The important lesson of totalitarian movements is that human power is generated not by advice but by dogma. Men are moved not by exhortation but by affirmations of the nature of their existence, wherein they are convinced of a unity between their own personal fulfilment and the march of events as a whole. Power comes from the unity of the inner and outer life which is induced by faith.'[1]

1. pp. 113, 119.

8

Pride and a Fall

DA *quod iubes*, prayed St Augustine, *et iube quod vis*. 'Give
what Thou commandest, and command what Thou wilt.' It is
a prayer that God is always more than ready to answer. He
commands nothing which (because He knows that of ourselves we cannot achieve it) He is not willing to give. And
what He gives is blessedness.

But why then is there that in me which rejects His gift? I
might well refuse to do all that was asked of me, if too much
seemed to be asked; but why should I refuse to have all done
for me? Yet that is just what is involved in rejecting the Gospel
of Christ. And, as I say, there seemed from the very beginning
to be that in me which desired to reject the Gospel. At the
same time, however, there was that in me which desired to
accept it, and for a time the issue was doubtful as between the
two contrary currents of desire. Gradually a decision was
reached, but alas! that is not yet dead in me which once
worked towards a refusal. 'For I delight in the law of God
after the inward man: but I see another law in my members,
warring against the law of my mind, and bringing me into cap-
tivity to the law of sin which is in my members.'[1]

What is it in us, then, which would have us reject the pro-
ferred divine salvation? It cannot, I am sure, be anything else
than *pride*. Only pride can account for our willingness to
receive from God a greater blessedness than we ourselves can
ever hope to win. Pride is thus the parent sin. It is at the root
of all that we call sin. In the myth of the Garden of Eden the
serpent's promise in tempting the first man and woman to sin
was 'Ye shall be as gods.'[2] The primary human temptation is

1. Romans 7: 22–3.   2. Genesis 3: 5.

the temptation to put ourselves in the place of God by claiming for ourselves a mastery of our own destiny which rightfully belongs to Him who is the Master of all destiny, and by seeking to do for ourselves that which He alone can do for us.

Some indeed have preferred to say that the essence of all sin is selfishness, while others, thinking of how difficult they find it to keep their body under and bring it into subjection, have said that it is rather sensuality. With the former of these statements I have little quarrel, and perhaps none at all if it be taken in a sufficiently wide sense, but the latter idea can be a most dangerous one, since it does but tempt us to another sinful evasion, namely, to throw the blame upon our bodies for a perverseness whose real seat is in our spirits. Our bodies are well enough – or would be if our spirits did not corrupt them. But it is much easier to see how selfishness and sensuality have their root in pride than to see how pride has its root in these. This may be understood in the following way. My contention has been that the fundamental fact of the whole spiritual life of man lies in his awareness of a transcendent authority under which he stands. He knows that he is not sovereign lord of his own life but is unconditionally subject to Another who alone is Sovereign Lord of all. I have testified that this was the first thing I myself knew, or was at least the common element in all my earliest knowings, and that ever since it has been the *only* element common to *all* situations in which I have ever been placed. Now it seems clear to me that all the muddle of mismanagement which I have allowed to creep into my life has arisen from my interference with this natural relationship between God and myself. I have mismanaged by trying to manage instead of letting God manage. Instead of letting His will be sovereign over mine, I have tried to exercise a sovereign will of my own. Not content with being dependent on Him, I have tried to assert my own independence. Deep down within me I always knew that He had His own plan for me, His own place for me, and in a sense even His own need of me; and I knew also that this plan, which was laid with a view to His sole glory, was laid also with a view to my own greatest happiness and welfare – because only in His glory could my happiness and welfare ever be found. But I was not content thus to allow the issues of my life to rest in His hands alone. I had certain little plans of my own. I wanted to arrange certain things a little differently. I thought I knew a thing or two about happiness, and about success, and I wanted to try out my own ideas. By so doing I put the whole nature of things out of joint. That which is in its proper nature subject I was making sovereign. That which is relative I was making absolute. I, a creature, was aspiring to independent creation.

It was only pride that could have made me do it, but it is easy to see how such pride had its first issue in selfishness. For what was I doing but putting self in the centre instead of God? Selfishness is indeed the form of sin which does most to poison the relation of man to man. And what an amazingly muddled spectacle our human society presents, with every one of us behaving with all but complete consistency as if all things had their centre in him! My first thought is for my own advantage, and yours (I hope I do you no injustice) is for yours. Or John Bull's first thought is for the interests of Britain and Uncle Sam's for the interests of America. There is no doubt, is there, that our trouble lies there? And if it does, it is small wonder that the trouble should be great. For the real world has only one centre, and how can we expect anything save the sorriest possible muddle if we attempt to give it as many centres as there are individual men or nations? The only centre of the real world is God. And until we recognize His centrality it were idle to hope for any alleviation of our present wretched plight.

Likewise the tempting notion that my body is the cause and seat of all the trouble finds here both its explanation and its necessary correction. My body is associated with sin only because it is so closely associated with *me*; but it is in me, that is, in my inmost self-conscious being, that sin has its real seat.

My body is the bit of externality that is nearest to me and the bit over which my spirit has most control. My body is the symbol of my particularity. Through it I am, as it were, tied down to a particular point in space and confined to a particular little span of time. Hence it may seem to be my body that influences me to destroy the true balance of things by judging all things in relation to myself, that is, making them relative to myself as absolute centre. I can, it is said, scarcely avoid seeing all things through the coloured spectacles of my own particular bodily passions and desires. There is just enough truth in this to make shallow thinkers overlook its numerous fallacies. The first fallacy lies in supposing my body to be the only source of the individuation of my spirit, as if my mind were not itself finite but were infinite mind constricted by its association with a finite bodily organization. The second fallacy lies in supposing that, because I am compelled to view all things from a single finite point of perspective, I am therefore compelled to regard this point as itself central. The third fallacy is in thinking of my passions and desires as merely bodily things, whereas in truth, and despite the obvious reference of some of them to bodily functions, they are themselves mental in nature. A fourth and closely related fallacy would arise if anybody were to speak, as hasty thinkers have often spoken, of my 'animal' passions and desires, and to hint that the sin in me is due to my animal ancestry. Of the many objections to this view, one that weighs much with me is that it so unjustly slanders the animals. 'A Bulgarian I met lately in Moscow', says one of Dostoyevsky's characters, 'told me of the crime committed by Turks and Caucasians in Bulgaria through fear of a general rising of the Slavs. They burn villages, outrage women and children, they nail their prisoners by the ear to the fences, leave them there until morning, and in the morning they hang them – all sorts of things you can't imagine. People talk sometimes of bestial cruelty, but that is a great injustice and insult to the beasts. A beast can never be as cruel as a man, as artistically cruel. The tiger only tears and gnaws; that is all he can do. But he would never think of nailing people by the ears, even were he able to do it.'[1] It is quite clear to me, then, that it is in the specifically human part of me that I must look for the source of my sinfulness, and not in anything that I have in common with the animals. 'There is no sin in the farm-yard.' Animal desire is not in itself evil; it only becomes evil when, in man, it seeks the aid of spirituality – of freedom and reason and the judgement of value – in order to convert its relativity into an absolute and its finitude into infinity. 'The impulses of nature', writes Professor Reinhold Niebuhr, 'only achieve demonic proportions when they are falsely "mixed" with spirit and gain immunity from the moral censor by appropriating the moral prestige of the spiritual.'[2]

It is, then, the pride in us that has put all things out of joint. Each of us behaves as if all things were centred in humanity and humanity in him. I *will* not see that I am no more important than the man next door. England *will* not see that she is no more important than her continental neighbours, or Germany that she is no more important than Poland or Czechoslovakia or Jewry. Man *will* not see that his importance lies not in himself but in his relation to God. And none of us is willing to understand that

> Our little systems have their day,
>   They have their day and cease to be,
>   They are but broken lights of Thee,
> And Thou, O Lord, art more than they.

Yet when man whose place is that of a servant thus sets himself up to be master, when he who was framed for obedience sets out to make his own independent plans, and especially when his pride leads him so to magnify the virtue of his own little doings and knowings that he forgets how all but bottom-

---

1. *The Brothers Karamazov*, Part II, Bk. V, Chapter iv.
2. *Reflections on the End of an Era*, p. 171.

less is his ignorance and how all but complete his impotence, then it is as if he had thrown a fatally hurtful piece of grit into the delicate web of relationship that alone binds him to the reality from which he draws his being. If such be the original sin of the human race, it is no wonder that the New Testament should say that its wages are death.

I shall therefore conclude this chapter with some further words of the same author whom I called to my help at the end of the last. 'This original sin is not something sub-human but a perversion of man's superiority to the process of becoming. It is that which makes us always tend to give objective value to our own particular interest and place in the stream of becoming, mistaking our own bias for the absolute truth or good; it is that which deceives us into erecting our own needs and our correction of other evils into schemes for saving the world; it is that which makes us paint in white and black the relative good we do and the evil we combat; it is that which sends us corporately from one false absolute to its dialectical opposite; it is that which moves us to fight for our prejudices as if we were fighting for God, or else to contract out of decision in the world unless we can envisage the choice as having unconditional divine warrant; it is that which bids us attribute others' evil to the malice of their free will and our own to the pressure of circumstances.'[1]

1. V. A. Demant, *The Religious Prospect*, p. 226 f.

9

Why We Cannot Put Ourselves Right

How is this hurt to be healed? Plainly it is futile to hope that we ourselves can heal it. If it is to be healed at all, it must be healed by God. Every attempt on my part to restore the proper order of things is likely only to make matters worse, since the root of the whole trouble lay in my original desire to order things by my own power, and this trouble will only be aggravated if I now seek to reorder them by my own power after they have once been disordered. It is impossible that the proud man should ever by his own efforts conquer his pride, since he would then be proud of having conquered it and would thus fall victim to the worst pride of all, namely, spiritual pride. Such spiritual pride is the sin that chiefly besets, not only the non-Christian forms of religion, but most of the defective forms of Christianity. The history of religion displays on almost every page the pathetic spectacle of men swollen in the conceit of their own self-abasement and self-immolation, and proud of their own humility. The spectacle presented by the history of humanism is not dissimilar, though sometimes it is more diverting than pathetic, as when in an autobiographical work published in the year 1930 I read the words, 'I have never lost the childlike humility which characterizes all truly great men'!

The temptation to believe that I can redeem myself after I have sinned is thus but a more insidious form of the temptation which originally led me to sin, namely, the temptation to regard myself as the maker of my own destiny. For it is plain that redemption, no less than creation, is a power that belongs to God alone. Only the Creator can redeem. Only the Maker can remake. *Qui fecit, refecit*, said St Augustine.[1] This is the

1. Epist. 231.

great realization that lies behind the Christian doctrine of Atonement, the main concern of which is to assert that, if we are to be saved from our sins at all, the conditions of our salvation must be provided by God Himself. 'O wretched man that I am!' cries St Paul, 'who shall deliver me from this body of death?' And his answer is, 'The law of the Spirit of life in Christ Jesus hath made me free from the law of sin and death. For what the law could not do, in that it was weak through the flesh, God sending his own Son in the likeness of sinful flesh, and for sin, condemned sin in the flesh: that the righteousness of the law might be fulfilled in us, who walk not after the flesh, but after the Spirit.'[1] Such a declaration embraces in itself far more aspects and facets of the Christian faith than can here even be touched upon, but at least it means this – that none of us can ever save himself by his own efforts.

The tragedy of our human situation, and the impossibility of relieving it save through an Atonement provided by God Himself, lies in the fact that we men, having once fallen into the sin of pride, are so infected and corrupted by it that we cannot conquer it without at once becoming proud of our conquest, and that even if we could, we would then in turn be proud of having conquered our pride without taking pride in the conquest, and so on *ad infinitum*. It is this endlessly regressive character of human sinfulness which makes the problem insoluble from our human end. The fact that my sin has this character is another proof that its seat is not, as Plato wrongly thought, in the lowest part of me but in the highest part of me, so that (as has often been observed) my worst defects are the defects of my highest qualities. For such infinite regressiveness is the very essence of that spiritual power which alone raises me above the brutes: it is the very essence of self-consciousness and the very definition of free will. To say that

1. Romans 7: 24; 8: 2–4. It must be borne in mind that 'flesh' in St Paul does not mean the body; it means human nature as at present constituted.

I am self-conscious means that I can survey myself from a point above myself; but if I can do that, then I can also, in due turn, survey the self that surveys as well as the self that is being surveyed; and then again I can survey the self that surveys the self that surveys; and so on without end. But if self-consciousness is the name of my glory, it is the name also of my shame. If it lies at the root of my superiority to the brutes, it lies also at the root of that sin which can drag me lower than the lowest brute. In our common speech self-consciousness is thus a term of reproach. To say that a man is self-conscious is to say something bad of him. This means that the self-consciousness which we actually find among men is always to some extent a perverted self-consciousness. None of us can think of himself without thinking of himself as occupying the centre of the stage. Thus the endless power of self-transcendence, which is our highest endowment, becomes changed into the equally endless and inescapable temptation to self-esteem which is the cause of all our woe.

There seems indeed to be no point at which my spiritual life does not fall victim to this infinitely regressive character of sin. I no sooner become aware of my pride than I become proud of being aware of it; and then if I reproach myself for this second sin, I go on at once to commit a third – I become proud of being aware of being aware of it. The same difficulty haunts me even in my devotions, perhaps indeed never more than in my devotions. I cannot confess my pride without being proud of my virtue in confessing. No sooner is the grace of true confession given me than I corrupt it by regarding the gift as if it were an achievement. I grow egotistic over the very discovery of my egotism. I read that Socrates was the wisest man in Athens because he alone of all the Athenians knew that he knew nothing, and I am tempted to conclude that, hopeless egotist as I am, I at least differ from the common run of egotists in being virtuously aware of the extent of my egotism; yet clearly if I so argue, I am *not* yet aware of the extent of my egotism. Or again, I grow sinfully self-confident over the very discovery of my sinful self-confidence. I have come to realize my own helplessness and inability to make any contribution to my salvation; yet since this realization alone makes it possible for me to entrust my whole salvation to Christ alone, I begin to think that I have made at least *this* contribution to my own salvation, namely that, unlike *some* people I could mention, I am at least aware of my own inability to contribute to it; and thereby I prove more conclusively than ever that I am *not* aware of my own inability to contribute to it. I remember being told in New York of a Sunday School teacher who concluded a lesson on the parable of the Pharisee and the Publican by saying, 'And now, children, let us thank God that we are not as this Pharisee.'[1]

Here again, as it seems to me, is the tragedy of the forlorn attempts that our too self-conscious, or rather pervertedly self-conscious, modern world is making to recapture something of the more objectively-conditioned consciousness of an older day. And, if I may make Mr T. S. Eliot's definition my own, 'When I say "modern mind", I mean the minds of those who have read or could have read such a document as Rousseau's *Confessions*.'[2] How we moderns strive for sincerity, and in what coils of subtler insincerity do we become entangled in the process! I think of one good friend of mine whose whole life is a passionate quest for absolute sincerity. He is all the time torturing himself in the attempt to cut his way through the successive layers of pretence which seem to him to stand, as it were, between his 'I' and his 'Me', overlaying his real self, and interfering with his knowledge of his real thoughts and motives. But to listen to him is like watching a man trying to peel an onion so as to reach the core. One feels that the process is inherently self-defeating and *cannot* succeed. There is always some insincerity involved in every human attempt to be

1. Cf. Luke 18: 11.
2. *Selected Essays*, p. 258.

sincere. Again the regress is endless. Sincerity does *not* lie at the core. It does not lie in me. It lies in God, who alone is faithful and true.

So far I have been speaking of the problem of salvation as if it were mainly a problem of overcoming the *power* of sin in our lives, but that is plainly not the whole of the problem, since there is also the question of overcoming the guilt of it. The familiar hymn says,

> Be of sin the double cure,
> Cleanse me from its guilt and power.

And there is every reason to believe (as has been well brought out in Mr Eliot's play, *The Family Reunion*) that the ravages wrought by the sense of guilt are no less in the modern soul than they were in the ancient, and that the denizens of our brave new world are no less disturbed by it than were King Oedipus or Mary Magdalene or Lady Macbeth themselves, however different an account they may give of it to themselves, so that they are sometimes led to carry the symptoms of it to the psychoanalyst rather than to the priest. But men have always known that what guilt needs is expiation or atonement, and the men of today know that too, and show by their behaviour that they know it, though they will not always admit to the knowledge and sometimes even elaborately deceive themselves into thinking that they do not know it. Men who have something on their consciences will usually be found trying to *make up* for whatever it is they have done or omitted to do; and such making up is just what is meant by atonement and expiation. And how pathetic a spectacle is often presented by this business of trying to make up for our past misdeeds! For once again the seeds of defeat lie in the very nature of the effort. I try to compensate for having done less than my duty in the past by doing more than my duty in the future. But alas! there exists nothing that is more than my duty. 'We are unprofitable servants: we have done that which was our duty to do.'[1] Of course, it is true that in the sphere of merely contractual relationships I can exceed my obligation, so that if last week I paid less than my due, I can make up for it by paying more than my due this week. But if any moral element should enter into the situation, if the obligation should not be merely contractual in nature but in some degree also moral, then such compensation becomes impossible, since moral obligation is of its very nature absolute and unconditional. If, for instance, I thought to *cheat* you by paying less than my proper instalment last week, then I cannot cancel *this* wrong that I have done you by paying a larger instalment this week – not even should I now be able to pay *more* than is necessary to make up the pecuniary loss you previously incurred. No payment can compensate for a breach of confidence. We are here in the region, not of limited legal contracts, but of personal relationships. We are dealing not with law but with love. A more suitable example than that of creditor and debtor would therefore be that of a man and his wife. A man who has been unkind to his wife often tries to 'make up' for his unkindness by being now – how shall I put it? – even kinder than it is necessary to be. But the attempt is foredoomed to failure, for there is no limit to the kindness which it is 'necessary' for a man to show to his wife. The demands of love are without limit, for to let love degenerate into sentimentality is a very different feat from the impossible one of letting love overflow its own bounds.

The attempt to atone for defection from duty in the past by exceeding our duty in the future is, however, also blocked for us by a difficulty of a more practical kind – the difficulty that such an attempt to cleanse myself from the *guilt* of sin presupposes that I have already been delivered from its *power*, whereas in truth I cannot be delivered from its paralysing power while its guilt still weighs upon me. Even if there did exist some kind of service that went beyond my duty, how

1. Luke 17: 10.

should I, who have hitherto been unable to do as much as is my due, now be able to do more than is my due? Such a doctrine is a counsel of pure despair. It does but trifle with the realities of the situation with which it professes to deal. Your moralizings do not even touch my real need. Had I been able to do even what was incumbent on me, I should not have troubled you with my affairs at all; how ironic must therefore sound your advice that my best course is now to do more than is incumbent on me! Indeed it is doubly idle of you to suggest that I should compensate for past failure by future excess of merit, seeing that the very failure has worked further havoc with my will power, leaving me one degree more impotent than I was before. That is why any radical cure of sin must be, as the hymn says, a 'double cure' that tackles the problem of guilt at the same time as it tackles the problem of power. For while my sin retains its power over me, I have no power to accomplish anything that might atone for its guilt. Clearly, then, I can do nothing to earn that reconciliation with God in which alone my salvation lies. If only I *were* reconciled, I might be able to do something in the strength of the encouragement so accruing; but while I remain unreconciled, the necessary strength and courage are lacking. A man who through constant bickerings with his wife has caused a breach in the good understanding between them, and so spoiled his marriage, will often try to put matters right by now behaving as a model husband and so earning a right to be reconciled. But the difficulty is that, until the relationship has already been restored, he lacks the conditions necessary to his behaving as a model husband, since a model husband's behaviour towards his wife is founded upon mutual confidence and understanding and becomes an entirely artificial thing – becomes merely 'model' behaviour in the bad sense – when the attempt is made to build it upon any other foundation. Reconciliation cannot then be earned by self-improvement, since self-improvement is itself only possible on the basis of a reconciliation already accomplished.

Moreover, the attempt to earn forgiveness by improved behaviour is likely to defeat its own end in another way still. Such attempts at self-justification are more likely to alienate than to reconcile. The plea, made in humble self-abasement, to be taken back 'just as I am', and to be given another chance, is much more likely to succeed. My wife is not interested in model behaviour that is consciously intended to placate her; what she wants is love, and that spontaneous and unselfconscious good behaviour which is the natural result of love. And so it is also in my relation with God. What has gone wrong in that relation can never be put right by any attempt at self-justification on my part, nor by any attempt to be worthy of His forgiveness or to earn it by efforts at self-improvement which can have no effect but that of concentrating my attention on myself instead of Him. That is why Christianity teaches that salvation is not by works but by faith, and that 'justification' is a pre-condition of sanctification and not a result of it. We cannot put ourselves right with God by being good; we can only be good when we are already right with Him; and therefore we must be put right by Him and not by ourselves.

All this has been so well argued in a little book by Mr Lesslie Newbigin that I shall venture to quote from it the following sentences, as serving to sum up much of what I have tried to say. 'We are going to do better tomorrow to make up for today; we are going to do good deeds, not because they are good, but to justify ourselves. A fundamental selfishness has got into the very heart of our motives. We have introduced just that seed of egocentricity which turns free spontaneous self-forgetting goodness into "good works" done with an ulterior motive.... But we have not only corrupted moral motives. We have also lowered moral standards. For if we suppose, as a legalistic morality constantly does, that we can make up for past failure by extra efforts in the future, we are acting on the assumption that it is possible to have a sort of credit balance in goodness – in other words, that it is possible to do more than our duty. If I suppose that my goodness today is going to compensate for my failure yesterday, I am really supposing, as far as today is concerned, that I can be better than necessary.... But there is yet a third peril besetting the moral life.... We have considered the peril of self-justification. There is also the peril of self-sanctification. This also may be stated in one paradoxical sentence: while the most important thing about a man is character, not good deeds, yet to make the improving of character the direct aim of our actions corrupts morality.... To make the improving of our own character our central aim is hardly the highest kind of goodness. True goodness forgets itself and goes out to do the right for no other reason than that it is right.'[1]

1. *Christian Freedom in the Modern World*, pp. 24–7.

10

How We May be Put Right

'In those days it shall come to pass that ten men from nations of every language shall take hold of the shirt of one Jew, saying, We will go with you, for we have heard that God is with you.'[1] The words are those of Zechariah the prophet, and they have come true in a wider sense than even he was able to foresee. For countless men and women of every race and tongue and nation the story of the Jews is now sacred history and the land of the Jews is their Holy Land. Why is this?

It is because from this history and this land there has come to us the mending of our human situation, the atonement for our sin, and the cure for our pride. We have seen how impossible it was, in the very nature of the case, that we should ourselves provide this cure and atonement and mending. It had to be provided by God or not at all. And it has pleased God, in the unsearchable counsel of His will, that He should provide it in this particular context of time and place and race, so that the Saviour of the world should be of Nazareth and 'a rod out of the stem of Jesse'.[2]

If we take the Bible literature as a whole, what do we find that it amounts to? The answer is really quite simple. It amounts to the revelation that what we could not do for ourselves God, in His infinite love and mercy, has done for us. In a famous passage of his *Varieties of Religious Experience* William James says that however widely the various religions of the world may differ from one another, there are two things they all have in common – 'a sense that there is something wrong about us as we naturally stand' and 'a sense that we are saved from this wrongness by making proper connexion with

1. Zechariah 8 : 23.   2. Isaiah 11 : 1; Romans 15 : 12.

the higher powers'.[1] In the various religions there may indeed be some adumbration of a satisfying conception of the 'higher powers' and a 'proper connexion' with them. But only in the Christian Gospel is the depth of our wrongness really met, because indeed it is only there that the depth of our wrongness is truly understood. What we now learn is that the burden of this wrongness has been wholly borne by God Himself. It is not that by 'making proper connexion with Him' we can put right our wrongness – hitching our wagon to a star. For then again the achievement would in part be our own, and the pride we had driven out of the front door would come in by the back. It is rather that, wrong as we are, and even wrong as we shall continue to be, He has put all things right. Our salvation consists in trusting and rejoicing in His rightness rather than in trying to put ourselves right. The Christian revelation is that God accepts me 'just as I am', and not because I have first become other than I am. I am saved when my delight in His perfect righteousness raises me above my despair over my own sin. 'Therefore we conclude', says St Paul, 'that a man is justified by faith without the deeds of the law',[2] and I am saved 'not having mine own righteousness, which is of the law, but that which is through the faith of Christ, the righteousness which is of God by faith.'[3] In this way, and in this way alone, can the vicious circle be broken and the infinite regress of human pride reach its term. 'Where is boasting then?' asks St Paul. 'It is excluded.'[4] If, wrong as I am, I am saved by a rightness which is not my own, there is nothing here on which my pride can feed.

It will be observed that such a way of salvation begins by tackling the guilt of my sin rather than its power over my will, and offers me forgiveness before it offers me holiness. Instead of being empowered to be a better man in order that I may thus be fit for acceptance with God, I am accepted 'just as I am' and

1. p. 508.   2. Romans 3 : 28.
3. Philippians 3 : 9.   4. Romans 3 : 27.

without being fit; and it is my acceptance while still unfit that alone has power in it to begin to make me fit. I am not saved because I have become sinless; I am saved, while still a sinner, because Christ is sinless and because He, being sinless, bare my sins in His own body on the Tree. But this being saved while still a sinner is the beginning of my ceasing to be a sinner, since the very substance of my sin was pride, and nothing can be so destructive of pride (or can, as St Paul says, so effectively exclude boasting) as to find oneself saved in such a way as this. To accept the fact of my own insincerity, to present myself to God for acceptance in all my insincerity but clothed in Christ's honesty, and in all my vanity but clothed in Christ's humility – such is the only way in which deliverance from insincerity and vanity can ever begin to come to me. It can only come if I believe that I am saved whether it comes or not. It is only on the basis of the justification of my still unsanctified self that my sanctification can begin. 'For by grace are ye saved through faith, and that not of yourselves: it is the gift of God: not of works, lest any man should boast. For we are his workmanship, created in Christ Jesus unto good works, which God hath before ordained that we should walk in them.'[1]

Such sanctification means that I am now endowed with righteousness or virtue of my own, as distinct from the righteousness of Christ whereby I am justified and forgiven. But it is a righteousness of a peculiar kind, a righteousness little understood by those who have not known Christ, a righteousness as different from the Jewish righteousness 'which is of the law' as from the characteristic virtues of the ancient classical world. It is a righteousness which consists in humility. 'Blessed are the poor in spirit.... Blessed are they that mourn. ... Blessed are the meek.... Blessed are they which do hunger and thirst after righteousness....'[2] – these are the Christian virtues, the elements of Christian saintliness. Because Christian

1. Ephesians 2: 8–10.   2. Matthew 5: 3–6.

sanctification means the progressive defeat of pride, it must mean gradual growth in humility.

The fact that the process is at best a gradual one means that, though forgiven, I still remain a sinner, and that, although saved from the guilt of sin, I am not yet saved from its power over my will.

> Let no man think that sudden in a minute
>   All is accomplished and the work is done; –
> Though with thine earliest dawn thou should'st begin it,
>   Scarce were it ended in thy setting sun.[1]

But how far may it be hoped that this gradual process should go within this present life? What measure of holiness may I hope to attain? And is *some* measure of holiness a necessary ingredient of *any* truly Christian state of soul, in addition to the knowledge that one's lack of holiness has been forgiven? These are perhaps as searching questions as it is possible to put to ourselves, and it is in the answers they have given to them that the different Christian communions have differed most widely from one another. It will be worth while to set out these differences shortly, even if this be something of a digression from the main course of our argument.

The Roman Church of the Middle Ages did not very clearly distinguish between justification and sanctification, and therefore did not sufficiently stress the priority of the former to the latter. It was the great contribution of the Protestant Reformation to insist on this priority, and what I have myself said about it here has been said under the influence of the Protestant tradition. It was Martin Luther who clearly taught me that I am *simul iustus et peccator*, at once saved and a sinner – though Luther was but underlining and recovering something that he had found in the New Testament. 'There is a sense', writes the Master of Balliol, 'in which no man is a Christian – the paradoxical sense that a man is a Christian only when he acknow-

1. F. W. H. Myers, *Saint Paul.*

ledges that he is not completely one.'[1] But perhaps Luther himself and certainly some of his followers have sometimes developed this true teaching in too one-sided a way. In their zeal for the recognition of justification, they have laid too little stress on the necessity of sanctification. In reading some Lutheran works one has the feeling that they are occupied too exclusively with the burden of sin's guilt upon the conscience, and are too little concerned with the continued power of sin's hold over the will. For Luther, writes one historian, 'to be saved by grace means not ... to be transformed by divine activity, but simply to be forgiven and restored to the divine favour.'[2] 'Divine forgiveness had, of course, always been regarded as an element in salvation. Luther, for the first time, made it the whole of salvation.'[3] Now clearly forgiveness is more than merely one element in salvation, it is the prime element which conditions all that follows; yet there is something that must follow if salvation is to be complete. For the Middle Ages grace meant primarily an infused power proceeding from God; for Luther, it meant only God's undeserved favour towards the impotent.[4] In this change lies the whole strength of the Reformation, and yet it is possible to see that if it be carried through in too one-sided a way, another and opposite danger lies in our path – the danger of resting so complacently in the assurance of forgiveness that we cease to be sufficiently troubled about our lack of progress in holiness. As against any such tendency to complacency it must be very strongly insisted that lack of progress in holiness casts serious doubts upon the genuineness of our reception of forgiveness. In other words, a justification that does not issue in sanctification is no true justification at all. This is plainly implied in our Lord's teaching. 'Ye shall know them by their fruits. Do men gather grapes of

1. A. D. Lindsay, *The Two Moralities*, p. 61.
2. A. C. McGiffert, *Protestant Thought Before Kant*, p. 27.
3. *Ibid.*, p. 25 f.
4. N. P. Williams, *The Grace of God*, p. 78.

thorns, or figs of thistles? Even so every good tree bringeth forth good fruit; but a corrupt tree bringeth forth evil fruit. A good tree cannot bring forth evil fruit, neither can a corrupt tree bring forth good fruit.'[1] It will be noticed that our Lord does not say that men are judged (or justified) by their fruits, but only that they are known by them. Yet this is quite enough to disturb any over-complacent assurance of salvation. If a good tree cannot bring forth evil fruit, then I must ask myself whether my continued failure to become more holy does not indicate that my spiritual life is not yet set upon the sure foundation of reconciliation with God. One New Testament book goes further, the book which Luther naturally enough liked least, calling it in the Introduction to his German translation of the New Testament 'a right strawy epistle (*eyn rechte stroern Epistel*)',[2] namely, the Epistle of James. Here it does seem to be taught that some acquisition of holiness is not merely a necessary consequence of justification but even an essential part of it. 'Yea, a man may say, Thou hast faith, and I have works: show me thy faith without thy works, and I will show thee my faith by my works.... But wilt thou know, O vain man, that faith without works is dead? Was not Abraham our father justified by works, when he had offered Isaac his son upon the altar? Seest thou how faith wrought with his works, and by his works was faith made perfect? ... Ye see then how that by works a man is justified, and not by faith only.... For as the body without the spirit is dead, so faith without works is dead also.'[3] It is probable that, just as the divergency of thought on this point between St Paul and St James cannot entirely be smoothed out, so we ourselves should avoid all one-sided extremes and be content with a never-completely-resolved 'tension' between the two opposite truths that have here to be kept in mind. Only thus perhaps can we have

1. Matthew 7: 16–18.
2. First Edition, Wittenberg, September 1522.
3. James 2: 18–26.

assurance without complacency. It remains only to note that while the main development of Reformation thought estimates very lightly the possibility of the acquisition of holiness during this present life, some of the lesser Protestant sects, Quaker, Methodist, and others, made the very most of this possibility and tended to be 'perfectionist' – sometimes even to a greater degree than Medieval Catholicism had ever been.

The alternative here presented to our thoughts is excellently summed up in the following passage which I take pleasure in quoting from one of Professor Niebuhr's books. 'The question is whether the grace of Christ is primarily a power of righteousness which so heals the sinful heart that henceforth it is able to fulfil the law of love; or whether it is primarily the assurance of divine mercy for a persistent sinfulness which man never overcomes completely. When St Paul declared: "I am crucified with Christ; nevertheless I live, yet it is no more I that live but Christ that dwelleth in me," did he mean that the new life in Christ was not his own by reason of the fact that grace, rather than his own power, enabled him to live on the new level of righteousness? Or did he mean that the new life was his only intention and by reason of God's willingness to accept intention for achievement? Was the emphasis upon sanctification or justification?

'This is the issue upon which the Protestant Reformation separated itself from classical Catholicism.... If one studies the whole thought of St Paul, one is almost forced to the conclusion that he was not himself quite certain whether the peace which he had found in Christ was a moral peace, the peace of having become what man truly is; or whether it was primarily a religious peace, the peace of being "completely known and all forgiven", of being accepted by God despite the continued sinfulness of the heart. Perhaps St Paul could not be quite sure about where the emphasis was to be placed, for the simple reason that no one can be quite certain about the character of this ultimate peace. There must be, and there is, moral content in it, a fact which Reformation theology tends to deny and which Catholic and sectarian theology emphasizes. But there is never such perfect moral content in it that any man could find perfect peace through his moral achievements, not even the achievements which he attributes to grace rather than the power of his own will. This is the truth which the Reformation emphasized....'[1]

1. *Christianity and Power Politics*, New York (1940), p. 18 f.

I I

The Relevance of the Gospel

THE good news of Christianity is that God wrought salvation for us by becoming manifest in the flesh in 'the man Christ Jesus',[1] 'who his own self bare our sins in his own body on the tree, that we, being dead to sins, should live unto righteousness.'[2] In order to understand the nature of this manifestation Christian thought has had to frame its doctrine of the Holy Trinity. It could not hold that God the Father Himself came down to earth, as Zeus might do in a Greek story, and Himself suffered and died upon the Cross. God cannot suffer and die. It was Christ in His manhood who suffered and died. And yet Christian thought knew that in this human suffering and death God Himself was present and His love made manifest. This cannot be expressed save by means of the symbol that within the Divine Unity there is a Trinity of Persons, and that God the Father sent His Son to be united to our humanity and so to suffer and die for our sakes. About this mystery of the Trinity I cannot here say more; but it can never be understood save as an attempt to contain and express the Christian knowledge that in that particular context of Jewish history, in that little eastern land, and on that first Christmas Day now nearly two thousand years ago, there was born into our world 'a Rod out of the stem of Jesse', who was to work for us a salvation that we could not work for ourselves and no man could work for us, but only God Himself. The core of the doctrine of the Trinity is to be found in the conviction that 'God was in Christ, reconciling the world unto himself, not imputing their trespasses unto them.'[3]

There is, however, no doubt that since the period of the

1. Timothy 2: 5.   2. 1 Peter 2: 24.   3. Corinthians 5: 19.

Renaissance, and especially since the period of the *Aufklärung*,[1] many men have found a kind of difficulty in believing this such as had only rarely been felt during the previous fourteen or more centuries of Europe's history. Not that they have desired to deny the exceptional significance of the figure of Jesus of Nazareth. They have for the most part been anxious to give their assent to the Christian affirmations that He is the greatest of mankind, that His life is our highest pattern and His death the world's noblest martyrdom, and that His teaching is the highest and truest that the world has yet received. But the great central Christian affirmation to which these others are sub-servient, the affirmation that here as nowhere else was God Himself working out our salvation, coming down to earth for our sakes, taking on our humanity and taking upon Himself the whole burden of human sin – this they have found it diffi-cult to believe. Indeed it is probable that something of the kind of difficulty I have in mind is felt by the great majority of modern seekers after truth. Certainly I have myself been no stranger to it.

There is of course a kind of refusal to accept the salvation wrought by God in Christ which has been sadly familiar in every age, and the seat of which is not in the intellect but in the will. In all men there is a sinful unwillingness to be done with their sins and to let them, as it were, be taken over for good and all by God. I do not know that there is more of such un-willingness in the world of today than there was in what we have come to call the Ages of Faith. But in the Ages of Faith, however reluctant men might be to be saved by Christ, very few were able to doubt the truth of the Church's teaching that such salvation was actually available in Christ. Whereas nowa-days there are many who would fain believe this but cannot. It would be nothing but trifling with a serious subject to say, as some well-meaning folk still do, that these moderns differ from their forefathers only in being more wicked.

1. Or Enlightenment.

What then is the source of this new sort of difficulty in belief? It must clearly be looked for in the changed outlook on human life and history which came in with the Renaissance and was reinforced by the *Aufklärung*. This outlook may be very simply described: it was a new realization of the powers and dignity of man. Throughout the Ages of Faith man's life and lot on earth had been priced very low; the value they had was not intrinsic in themselves but lay only in their character as a probation and preparation for a very different life and lot beyond the grave. And there was equally little confidence in man's ability to better his lot on earth or to make his life other than it has always been. Now, however, men began to find, if I may borrow the lines of a much later versifer, that

> The world is so full of a number of things,
> I'm sure we should all be as happy as kings.

Our earthly life might or might not be a forecourt of eternity — and if it were, then its *main* significance must still be allowed to lie in its preparatory character: but in either case it was a sufficiently fascinating business in itself, full of interest and of all sorts of unexplored possibilities.

That this new humanistic outlook has brought us great gain nobody (who understands what he is saying) is likely to doubt. It has given us the culture and civilization of the modern West. It has given us the whole development of modern art and literature, from Michelangelo and Shakespeare downwards. It has given us modern scholarship and the whole conception of modern historical research. It has given us universal education. To it are due the triumphs of modern medicine and hygiene and the whole remarkable developments of modern science and technology. To it are due also the triumphs of modern travel and exploration, from Diaz and Columbus downwards. Beginning with the researches of Copernicus and Galileo and Kepler, it has changed for us our whole conception of the physical universe. Yet no less has it changed for us the order of our human society. Politically, it has been responsible for the replacement of the absolutism of the Holy Roman Empire by modern ideals of democracy and toleration and freedom of speech and the rights of the individual. Sociologically, it has been equally responsible for the whole modern hope of social reform. This is how the change is described in one well-known text-book: 'It was the bright dawn of human reason, the springtime of the soul. After a long and harsh winter, the earth sprang to new life under the kindly rays of the sun. A rich seed had been planted in it: now it bore a capricious but plentiful harvest, a vegetation which covered and hid the old soil, though supported by it; just as vigorous plants, springing from the foot of an old oak, embrace and protect it with their young roots. Everything was born again – art, science, philosophy – and the world, held fast for two centuries in the morass into which it had fallen during the Middle Ages, now travelled once more towards the light and the purer air of reason.'[1]

Yet these glowing words do not now carry the same conviction which they did when they were written in the nineteeth century. For, however impossible it is to doubt that the outlook of the Renaissance has brought us gain, there are few who are not now beginning to ask themselves whether it did not bring us loss as well. This we have already had occasion to note, remarking that our own time is characterized by nothing so much as by the threatened breakdown of the humanist mentality. Men are – to say the very least – much less sure than they once were that the culture and civilization of the modern West has been an unmixed blessing, and they are beginning to suspect that some kind of defect lay in the very roots of it, not in any mere incidents and accidents of its later growth.

In the very roots of it. These roots, we said, were a new belief in the power of man to order his own life, a new sense of

1. Victor Duruy, *A Short History of France*, tr. Jane and Menzies, Chapter xlii.

the dignity and interest of his earthly occupations, and a new hope for the future of his earthly society. But however beneficent in their workings such a hope and belief may be when kept within their own reasonable limits, it can readily be understood that they fall an easy prey to the characteristic sin of pride; and such is the fate that has now overtaken them. Had they been kept within proper limits, we could not only have equally well enjoyed the blessings of modern society, as contrasted with the society of the Dark Ages, but have looked forward to a much more secure tenure of these blessings; but instead of that they were quick to overreach themselves, and it is this that has led to disaster.

But now it is easy to understand how, to a humanity thus swollen in its own conceit, the Christian doctrine of salvation should have found increasing difficulty in commending itself. Let us endeavour to lay bare the anatomy of this difficulty. It is a task that must occupy us both in the present and in the following chapter.

In the first place, the new belief in man's power to control his own fate has made us less conscious of our need of a salvation wrought for us by God. This need not have happened if we had been careful accurately to delimit the measure of control which in the nature of the case was possible to us, but such carefulness was not found sufficiently flattering to our pride. Here is an example which will serve as a type of many others. René Descartes, the first great philosopher of the modern world, once wrote: 'If it should ever prove possible to find some means of making men gentler and wiser than heretofore, I believe that means will be found in medicine.'[1] There, at the very birth of modern thought, you have the whole matter in a nutshell! What an inestimable blessing humanism has brought us in modern medicine! How triumphantly have we demonstrated our power to better our human lot by the conquest of disease, the diminution of suffering and postponement of

1. See *The Times Literary Supplement* of 12 July 1934.

death! Even within so short and recent a period as the twenty years of peace between the two great world wars we have, according to Mr Walter Elliot, a former Minister of Health, 'more than halved the death-rate from consumption, halved the maternal mortality rate, halved the death-rate for small babies; and we have put three pounds of weight and half an inch in height on to the physique of the average school child between 1927 and 1937 alone.... We also moved a million people out of the slums.'[1] How successfully also have even some diseased *mental* conditions begun to be tackled by physical means, so that modern man goes to his doctor for worries that would have sent medieval man to his priest! But Descartes does not content himself with that; he hopes that medicine will also make men 'gentler and wiser'; which means that medicine is going to solve their spiritual problem too. And, as time passed, the hope that the progress of science and generally of modern civilization would bring about a fundamental improvement of our situation became ever bolder. In the nineteenth century we find John Stuart Mill writing: 'Most of the great positive evils of the world are in themselves removable and will, if human affairs continue to improve, be in the end reduced within narrow limits.... All the grand sources, in short, of human suffering are in a great degree, many of them almost entirely, conquerable by human care and effort.'[2] Mill accordingly found sufficient consolation in the salvation that man might work out for himself, and felt no need of the salvation that is in Christ. So also, in our own day, Mr George Bernard Shaw finds sufficient refuge in the dream of an improved human race whose average term of life will extend to three hundred years instead of three score years and ten. He thinks that would solve our deepest problems.[3] The late M. Bergson was bolder still and in the three unobtrusive words that close

1. See the daily press of 5 December 1940.
2. *Utilitarianism*, Chapter II.
3. See *Back to Methuselah*.

the third chapter of his *Creative Evolution* he even seemed to suggest that we may so far evolve creatively that an immortal race will one day be produced on earth by natural means. 'The animal', he prophesies, 'takes its stand on the plant, man bestrides animality, and the whole of humanity, in space and time, is one immense army galloping beside and before and behind each of us in an overwhelming charge able to beat down every resistance and clear the most formidable obstacles, perhaps even death.'[1]

An age dominated, or even infected, by such hopes and beliefs as these was hardly a favourable soil for the sower whose seed was the word of God in Christ. When the prospects for man's control of his own destiny seemed so bright, he could not be expected to lend a ready ear to the news that God had so intervened in human history as to take the whole rehabilitation of man's destiny upon Himself. Our own generation, however, has witnesed a very general decline of such roseate expectations, and it is precisely in its surrender of these false hopes that the hopefulness of the new age lies. Men are much less sure than they were a generation ago that science and civilization are ever going to save the world. They are prepared for an altogether more realistic stock-taking. They are asking themselves whether Western man has after all succeeded, or is ever likely to succeed, in making any essential difference to the tragic solemnity of his human situation, whether the deepest root of our common trouble has so much as been touched, and whether, after all has been done that human skill and science can devise, we are not still as perilously poised on this old planet as ever we were before, and still do not know what a day or an hour may bring forth. In such an atmosphere of realism 'the old, old story' has a much better prospect of being believed.

In the second place, and in most intimate connexion with what has just been said, we must note how much more *at home* modern man has seemed to find himself in the present world

1. *Op. cit.*, English translation, p. 285 f.

than did the men of earlier Christian centuries or even of the ancient classical world. Those forefathers of ours had ever a keen sense of the strangeness of their human situation and of their earthly environment. Such a sense pervades the Old Testament. 'Thy statutes', sings a psalmist, 'have been my songs in the house of my pilgrimage.'[1] 'I am a stranger in the earth: hide not thy commandments from me.'[2] He is lost and alone, therefore he longs for divine guidance and help. A New Testament writer declares that all the patriarchs of Israel 'confessed that they were strangers and pilgrims on the earth',[3] and another beseeches his readers 'as strangers and pilgrims, to abstain from fleshly lusts, which war against the soul.'[4] No perception lies closer than this to the root of New Testament thought, and it would not be difficult to show historically that the message of the New Testament succeeded in winning acceptance for itself only when, and so far as, men did feel themselves in this way to be, in the well-remembered Vulgate rendering, *peregrini et hospites super terram.*

It is recorded, for example, by the Venerable Bede that in the year A.D. 627, when the monk Paulinus was at the court of Edwin, King of Northumbria, endeavouring to persuade him to accept the Christian religion, the King was in two minds about it until one of his warriors addressed to him these famous and moving words: 'The present life of man upon earth, O King, seems to me, in comparison to the time which is unknown to us, like to the swift flight of a sparrow through that house wherein you sit at supper in winter with your ealdormen and thegns, while the fire blazes in the midst, and the hall is warmed, but the wintry storms of rain or snow are raging abroad without. The sparrow, flying in at one door and immediately out at another, whilst he is within is safe from the wintry tempest; but after a short space of fair weather he immediately vanishes out of your sight, passing from winter into winter

1. Psalm 119: 54.   2. Psalm 119: 19.
3. Hebrews 11: 13.   4. 1 Peter 2: 11.

again. So this life of man appears for a little while, but of what is to follow or what went before we know nothing at all. If therefore this new doctrine tells us something more certain, it seems justly to deserve to be followed.'[1] Thus was Edwin persuaded to receive baptism and to build the first York Cathedral as the central shrine of a Christian north of England.

What is it that has changed this intellectual disposition of things for the modern world, making it more difficult for men to believe in the Christian message which Paulinus brought to Edwin? Is it that a more careful scrutiny has thrown grave suspicion upon the truth and authenticity of the message? If it were merely that, the situation would be simpler, and I believe also that the prospects for a revival of Christianity would be more favourable – because the new-discovered objections to the validity of the Christian claim do not strike me as being by any means insuperable in themselves. But it is not merely the belief that God was in Christ that has failed, but also the need for the belief; and it would be trifling with the facts to suggest that the *simultaneous* failure of the belief and of the need of the belief was merely a strange coincidence; while we should be equally seriously misrepresenting the historical facts of the situation if we were content to say that it was because men were no longer able to believe that they now felt no need to believe. The reverse of this is much more like the truth. It is not the modern study of history which, resulting in a 'de-supernaturalization' of the Gospel story, has led to the confident humanistic estimate of our ability to solve our own problems and order our own lives; rather is it our confident humanism which has dictated our unbelieving philosophy of history. The appearance of a more optimistic assessment of human nature and a less tragic sense of our fallen and helpless estate is unmistakably the underlying factor in the situation. The beginnings of the sentiment that man is the master of his fate and captain of his soul can be traced much further back in

1. *Historia ecclesiastica gentis anglorum*, Lib. II, Cap. xiii.

the history of the development of *Aufklärung* than the specific doubt as to whether the New Testament claim for Christ is capable of substantiation. The failure of the sense of need is to a large extent responsible for the failure of the belief.

It is accordingly on the failure of the sense of need that we must concentrate our attention; and there is some ground for hope that if the sense of need could be revived in us, the ability to believe would revive in us also. But is not the sense of need already beginning to revive? Is Western man as sure today as he was only a little time ago that he can effect his own salvation? May it not be that in the tragic happenings of our time God is 'dealing with us as with sons',[1] in order that we may regain our lost knowledge of our own weakness and His power and will to save? Are there not already signs that men are feeling less wholly at ease upon earth than they lately thought themselves to be? Are there not those, even in some very unexpected quarters, who are beginning again to seek a Saviour and, in seeking, haply to find?

> Quam bonus te quaerentibus!
> Sed quid invenientibus?[2]

1. Hebrews 12: 7.
2. St Bernard of Clairvaux, *Jesu dulcis memoria*.

12

The Credibility of the Gospel

WE can thus understand how the prevailing humanism of the modern period has made the Gospel appear superfluous. But it has also made it appear unintelligible. How is this?

We must note, in the first place, that this modern humanism encourages us to regard history as a record of human initiative. It presents us with a picture of an upward-striving race. It tells us the story of a great quest, eagerly and relentlessly pursued, and resulting in conquests which, if still leaving much to be desired and many further heights to be attained, are nevertheless sufficiently remarkable if account be taken of the rude and low beginnings out of which they have emerged. It is for this reason that within the modern period so much has been made of the freedom of the human will. The earlier Christian ages did indeed also believe in the freedom of the will, but it was for a significantly different reason that they believed in it, and therefore it was a significantly different freedom in which they believed. They thought it important to believe in human freedom because they thought it important to believe in human *responsibility*. The point they were anxious to make was that man was free to *respond*. But the moderns have wanted rather to believe that man is free to initiate. The ancients felt they had to make man responsible for his sins; the moderns have been concerned rather to give him credit for his achievements. 'I'm a self-made man, you know,' explained a certain magnate of modern business to Dr Joseph Parker, who immediately replied, 'Sir, you have lifted a great load of responsibility from the Almighty.'

Now, for myself, I have long ago given up the attempt to fit the Christian Gospel into any such man-centred philosophy.

I am convinced that the attempt is hopeless. If free will represents the whole truth about human life, if our conquests are the fruit only of our own vitality and initiative, if our graces are the fruit only of our own decisions, and our knowledge the fruit of our own perspicacity – if, in short, the credit for all we have and are is fundamentally *our own* – then the Christian belief that God was in Christ is emptied of nothing less than the whole of its meaning. It was in the context of an entirely different reading of history that that belief first arose, and it is only in such a context that it can ever find intelligent acceptance. This different reading of history is, of course, the Bible reading of it, and it differs from the modern humanistic view *toto caelo* and from beginning to end. It begins by saying that God made man, whereas humanism prefers the view suggested by the title of a book by my brilliant colleague, Professor Gordon Childe, *Man Makes Himself*.[1] The Bible is throughout concerned with history, but it is history in which the chief actor is not man but God. It is God who rules the nations. It is God who determined the destiny of the children of Israel, with whose history the Bible is so much concerned. It is He who leads them out of Egypt, through the wilderness and into the promised land – they do not lead themselves! All their triumphs are represented as having been planned and conferred by Him. We are nowadays possibly prepared to regard these ancient Israelites as having possessed very great qualities. We say perhaps that as a race they were remarkably spiritually-minded. We say that we owe our religion to them. But such an attribution would greatly have astonished the Israelites themselves, who believed that they owed their religion wholly to God Himself. And what, think you, would the prophets of Israel have said, if it had been suggested to them that Israel was spiritually-minded or (as has been stated in many modern books) that she had 'a genius for religion'? They would have replied with stormy emphasis that Israel was, on the contrary,

1. 1936.

most obstinately carnally-minded and that, if she had what we call a 'genius' for anything, it was for apostasy and sin; but that nevertheless, and in spite of what she was, God had in His infinite mercy and loving-kindness chosen and ordained her to be the first-fruits of a redemption wrought by Himself alone. But surely, we protest, the Hebrew people *was* a highly gifted people and was endowed with many remarkable qualities? Yes indeed, but there we give ourselves away. We are using the terms of the Bible reading of history while emptying them of their proper meaning. For gifts are plainly things given and endowments are things conferred. Indeed it is surprising how great a difficulty free will finds in expressing itself in terms that do not imply predestination. The word 'genius' itself originally meant nothing less than a god, though it has now been wrested to the most man-centred of all uses.

Humanism has in this way attempted so to retell the story of the Old Testament as to make it no longer a record of divine grace and revelation but only a story of unaided human faith and discovery. Moreover it has even attempted to retell the story of the New Testament in this fashion, being sincerely anxious to retain as much of the traditional Christian message as it could by any means dovetail into its own outlook. Contemplating the figure of our Lord in its purely human aspect, it has often shown itself willing to place Him in the vanguard of our human progress, to regard Him as the spear-head of our human assault upon the unknown. He is, it is said, the great Trail-finder, the great Discoverer, our Leader in the forward march. In Him humanity attained. He had His human chance just as we have ours: He had His life to make or mar, and His human free will to make or mar it with. But He made more of His chance than any of the rest of us ever made of ours, using His free will to better ends. This is about the most that an anthropocentric humanism can admit, and (as we shall presently see) it often has very great difficulty in admitting even so much; and yet it is certain that if no more than this can be affirmed, then the whole glory has departed from the Christian religion. For this is neither what Christ believed about Himself nor what Christians have ever believed about Him. The Christian Gospel is that the will of *God* was responsible for all that was done in Galilee and in Jerusalem. The Christian Gospel is that God *sent* His Son into our history to be just what He was and to do just what He did. Christ is here set forth as the spear-head not of human but of divine enterprise; and He is set in the vanguard not only of the human quest for God but also of God's great quest of the human heart. 'I do nothing of myself,' said Christ, 'but as my Father hath taught me, I speak these things.'[1] Surely it stands at the utmost opposite extreme from an anthropocentric humanism, that One who claims to be Himself the Son of God should be found saying, 'I do nothing of myself'! 'I have finished the work which thou gavest me to do', He says again. '... Now they have known that all things whatsoever thou hast given me are of thee. For I have given them the words which thou gavest me; and they have received them, and have known surely that I came out from thee, and they have believed that thou didst send me.'[2]

The Christian confession concerning Christ cannot then be made to square with a purely free-will conception of human life and history, but only with the conception of human life and history as undergirded by the prevenient grace of God. And yet can we, in view of what has been before us in earlier sections, have any doubts as to which of the two conceptions more honestly reflects the facts? Can I, looking back on my own life and history, truthfully describe it as an eager quest? Was it I who was all the time seeking an elusive Good, or was I the elusive one, artfully evading a Good that was seeking me? And if haply there has been a finding, is it I who have at last found Him whom I sought, or is it He who has found me? Was I all that time knocking at His door or He at mine? Was it I who had the toil and trouble of the enterprise, or was it He? And

1. John 8:28.   2. John 17:4, 7–8.

shall the glory now be mine or His? Shall I sing of my achievement or of His gift? For me at least there can be but one answer.

> I sought the Lord, and afterward I knew
>> He moved my soul to seek Him, seeking me;
> It was not I that found, O Saviour true –
>> No, I was found by Thee.
>
> Thou didst reach forth thy hand and mine enfold;
>> I walked and sank not on the storm-vexed sea, –
> 'Twas not so much that I on Thee took hold,
>> As Thou, dear Lord, on me.
>
> I find, I walk, I love, but O the whole
>> Of love is but my answer, Lord, to Thee;
> For thou wast long beforehand with my soul,
>> Alway Thou lovedst me.[1]

If this is the answer I must return for my personal history, it is also the answer I must return for universal history. In the wider realm as in the narrower I shall expect to find, not an unflagging human quest for a God who does nothing except passively wait until He is found, but an active divine enterprise for the redemption of a humanity which, though indeed fitfully aware of its need of such redemption, proves none the less strangely unwilling to embrace it when it is offered. And in returning this answer, I shall be relieved of at least one typically modern difficulty in believing that God was in Christ, reconciling the world unto Himself.

There is, however, a second aspect of the humanistic interpretation of history that still falls to be considered as placing a stumbling-block in the way of this central Christian belief, namely, its conception of history as progress. We have already devoted some attention to this aspect of the thought of the

1. Anonymous verses which have been set to music, and are frequently sung, in America.

Aufklärung, but we must now look into the matter a little more closely.

The different views that have, during the course of history, been taken concerning its nature are not very many in number. They seem indeed to reduce themselves to five simple types, that is, five different patterns into which the course of events has been conceived by different people to fall. The first view is that of savages and uncivilized peoples among whom there is usually no consciousness of the course of events having shown, or being likely to show, any important variation from age to age, so that the pattern of history can be represented only by a horizontal straight line. The second view is that of the ruder civilizations, which have some sense of the ups and downs of history; and all we need do to represent their conception of the pattern of it is to replace the straight horizontal line by a wavy one. The third view is that which, in one or other of its forms, has mainly dominated the higher civilizations of the world, both Eastern and Western – the view which represents history as a circle or wheel, the same general cycle of events being repeated again and again, and the world returning periodically to the same original state. It is not without significance that this view has lately made several reappearances within our own civilization, when some have found it difficult to retain their belief in either of the two views which now remain to be described.

The fourth view is that which we find in the Bible, especially from the time of the great prophets downwards, and probably nowhere outside the Bible and the Jewish and Christian traditions, except in the religion of the Persians who were conquerors of the Jews and by whom Jewish thought may to some extent have been influenced in this matter. It is an altogether more complex and subtle view than any of the others, and is accordingly more difficult to state briefly or to represent graphically. It is a tragic view of history this, as some versions of the cyclical view had also been; but it looks forward to a final triumph, and in this it is quite original, differing from all views that preceded it or were contemporary with it or have ever been independent of it. In some of the latest parts of the Old Testament and in the whole of the New this triumph is regarded as constituting the end of history and as therefore being itself beyond history, if history be understood to mean the familiar course of our earthly life.

It was to men who worked with this view of history that the Christian Gospel of Incarnation and Atonement was first preached; when it was preached to the Greeks a little later by St Paul, this view of history was preached along with it; and it is only in conjunction with, and in the context of, this view of history that it can ever be intelligently accepted. History, as the Gospel sees it, begins with God's creation of man in His own image and man's fall from this high estate through pride. This beginning is, however – like all true beginning and ending – itself beyond history; for history is but the on-going of things between the beginning and the end. For this reason we are unable to represent it to ourselves save in symbolic or mythical dress, as with the garden and the snake, the rib and the apple. The Old Testament is, however, pervaded by the hope of a restoration, and slowly the idea begins to take shape that God will one day send a Saviour to inaugurate among His people a new Kingdom of righteousness and peace. The Christian Gospel is that Jesus of Nazareth was this Saviour; therefore Christians now no longer live in expectation of the Saviour's coming, as did the Jews (and as still do some of them); but look back to an Advent already manifest and rejoice in a salvation already procured, while waiting still in hope for a Second Advent, and for the full fruition of this salvation, in an eternal reign of glory which is beyond history also, at the other terminus of it.

The fifth view is that which regards history as a more or less continuous upward progress; having perhaps its ups and downs but showing in its general trend a steady ascent. This view may therefore be represented by means of a wavy sloping line which may be extended indefinitely in either direction. History, it is now believed, began very low down very long ago, it has now reached a height which is already most remarkable in view of its low beginnings, but its curve is still mounting rapidly, and most assuredly there lie ahead of us heights upon heights that are still undreamed. This view is a purely modern one. The first foreshadowings of it are probably to be set as far back as the seventeenth century, but it was not until the period of the *Aufklärung* that it found distinct and full expression. It was afterwards powerfully reinforced by the nineteenth-century doctrine of evolution which enabled it to express itself in a new and bolder form, yet that doctrine was itself rather a fruit of the idea of progress than the original root from which it sprang. Radically as this view diverges from the Bible view of history, it is in a certain sense dependent upon it, and it is no accident that it originated within a civilization which had in an earlier age been dominated by the Bible view. For all the other and earlier views of history the Bible view alone has this in common with the doctrine of progress – that it finds in history a direction and a purpose, that it looks forward expectantly, that it inspires men with the hope of more glorious things to come.

It is difficult to realize, and almost impossible to exaggerate, the extent to which our recent way of thinking has come to be dominated by this conception of progress, especially perhaps in its evolutionary form. We may find a type of this – and it is only one of many such that might be suggested – in the fact that the word *primitive*, which originally meant nothing more than *early*, is now taken to mean *rude*. This is exactly the doctrine of progress, that the early in date is the rude in quality, while the late in date is the noble and exalted. There was a day when primitive was a term of praise, as in 'the primitive Church' and 'the Primitive Methodists'; whereas now it is a term of disesteem, as in 'primitive peoples', 'primitive civilization,' and also (when the phrase was first so used) 'the Primitives' as meaning the painters before (very significantly) the Renaissance.

Now I am quite sure that one important part of the modern difficulty of believing in the Christian scheme of salvation is simply the impossibility of fitting it into the context of such a progressivist view of history. Nor is this merely because such a view encourages a human pride which dulls our sense of the need of salvation and an over-sanguine optimism for which the Cross is only a stumbling-block and a rock of offence. Both of these things are true, but they have already sufficiently engaged our attention, whereas the special difficulty which inheres in the doctrine of progress has not yet engaged our attention. We have seen that modern anthropocentric humanism, since it regards history as a record of the results of human initiative, has found it hard to accept the Christian view of Christ as sent by God, or as being Himself God come down to earth, for our salvation, and yet has frequently been willing to regard Him as the greatest of mankind, the ideal pattern of humanity and the teacher of the highest truths that we know. But we must now note that the humanism of the last hundred and fifty years has frequently found it difficult to allow even this. Many examples could be cited of modern writers straining their progressivist premises almost to breaking-point, and in all sincerity torturing themselves into a final insincerity, in the attempt to retain this slender hold upon the Christian tradition. Their difficulty has been that of understanding how the climax of an upward process that is still going on could have come two thousand years ago. For the Christian view Christ is the centre of history; but what can be meant by the centre of an infinite ascending line? How could Christ on the Cross have said 'It is finished', if the tale of modern progress had by that time hardly begun? How is a scheme which divides human story into B.C. and A.D. to be made congruent with a doctrine that knows only the distinction between ruder and more advanced? And if the best is still to be, how then can we look backwards in time to a Pattern and Exemplar, or to the final revelation of truth?

I am not, indeed, going to suggest that we should solve this problem for ourselves by altogether jettisoning the idea of progress from our minds. I have already expressed my conviction that the protest entered by the humanism of the Renaissance against the outlook of the so-called Ages of Faith was in part necessary and justified, containing precious perceptions of truth which must be built into the Christianity of the future; and I have said that, like the Renaissance, the *Aufklärung* also stands not alone for grievous errors whose bitter fruits we are now reaping, but for gains which we are now struggling to conserve and to defend against the assaults of latter-day irrationalisms and totalitarianisms. The modern belief in progress is an essential part of the outlook of the *Aufklärung*, and of it also the same holds true. It has brought much blessing to mankind. It has provided initiative for improvements of our earthly lot and for reforms of our earthly society such as could not have come about in a less sanguine age. In certain narrow fields, at least, important progress has actually been recorded during the last hundred and fifty years; and this progress not only provides partial justification for the belief in progress but is itself a fruit of that belief and could never have taken place apart from the inspiration it provided.

But the tragic error of the progressivism of the *Aufklärung*, no less than of the humanism of the Renaissance, lay in its independence of God. To such an outlook one must apply the words of Bailie Nicol Jarvie to Rob Roy in the inn at Aberfoyle, 'An they ken naething better than that, they had better no ken that neither.'[1] The Christian teaching has always been that human freedom can arise only out of bondage to God, that human initiative should exist only as a response to the divine initiative, and that true growth is possible only on the basis of

1. Scott, *Rob Roy*, Chapter xxxiv.

repentance and the acceptance of a salvation wrought by God alone. Since man is a fallen creature, progress without an initial repentance can only be progress in sin. All true growth must either be growth in grace or, if growth in other things than grace, then growth upon a foundation which grace has laid; and faith must precede works. This the Ages of Faith knew well. Their defect was the opposite one of laying insufficient emphasis upon the freedom that might be combined with this ultimate subservience, and upon the degree of human initiative and reformatory power that might thus be encouraged. It was this defect which gave the Renaissance its opportunity, an opportunity which it partly misused. The problem of the present day is to recover our Christian heritage without allowing the very real gains of the Renaissance and *Aufklärung* to be swallowed up in the pessimism and unreason of a new Dark Age, that is, to regain our sense of dependence upon God without again surrendering our sense of human freedom or extinguishing human initiative and reformatory zeal. Our humanism, if it is to survive, must find its ultimate centre and inspiration not in man but in God, and its hope for the future must be a hope not in ourselves but in Him. If we are still to believe in progress, it must be a progress based neither in ourselves nor (as in evolutionism) in nature, but in the Supernature which is God.

The threatened collapse in our time of the whole structure of modern thought as built up by the Renaissance and *Aufklärung* is something that may well give rise in our breasts to the greatest disquiet and alarm, yet we cannot fail to find in it also a nemesis, or rather – to use a more Christian phrase – a judgement of God. God's judgements are, however, intended to lead us, not to despair, but to repentance and an amendment of our ways; and signs are not lacking that the series of severe jolts which have lately been suffered by those who have supported their spirits by the hope of a natural and necessary upward progress of our earthly society is actually leading some of them to open their minds more hospitably to what I have called the Bible view of history. 'In the whole of the New Testament, Gospels and Epistles alike', writes Professor Niebuhr in the context of the passage already quoted from him, 'there is only one interpretation of world history. That pictures history as moving towards a climax in which both Christ and anti-Christ are revealed. The New Testament does not, in other words, envisage a simple triumph of good over evil in history. It sees human history involved in the contradictions of sin to the end. That is why it sees no simple resolution of the problem of history. It believes that the Kingdom of God will finally resolve the contradictions of history; but for it the Kingdom of God is no simple historical possibility. The grace of God for man and the Kingdom of God for history are both divine realities and not human possibilities. The Christian faith believes that the Atonement reveals God's mercy as an ultimate resource by which God alone overcomes the judgement which sin deserves. If this final truth of the Christian religion has no meaning to modern men, including modern Christians, that is because even the tragic character of contemporary history has not yet persuaded them to take the fact of human sinfulness seriously.'[1]

But some of us are, I think, beginning to be persuaded; and with this we are beginning to think ourselves out of the four habits of humanistic thought which I have now enumerated (two in this chapter and two in the preceding one) and which I believe to be the principal causes of our modern intellectual difficulty with the full Christian confession about Christ. For some at least the disappointment of their too sanguine and too secular hope for the progress of the earthly city has, by the grace of God, removed a serious stumbling-block from the path of their pilgrim's progress towards the Celestial City. It has inclined their minds to entertain once more the Christian belief that, at a certain particular time and in a certain particu-

1. *Christianity and Power Politics*, pp. 20-1.

lar place, our earthly history has been invaded by a divine
enterprise of salvation. Once more, then, they can address
their Lord and sing,

> Be Thou my Shield and Hiding-place,
> That, sheltered near Thy side,
> I may my fierce accuser face
> And tell him Thou has died.[1]

1. John Newton's 'Approach, my soul, the mercy-seat'.

13

Journey's End

WHEN I reflect on the difficulties which once beset my own mind in regard to the intellectual acceptance of the Christian message of salvation, it is fairly clear to me that their deepest root lay in such exaggerated estimates of our human ability and of the possibilities of our planetary existence as I have now set out; for there is hardly any chance of the New Testament teaching being made to seem reasonable to minds which, while being otherwise of an inquiring disposition, remain complacently satisfied with the prospects of self-improvement confronting either themselves as individuals or our earthly society as a whole.

What the Gospel offers to do for me is to set me at peace with God, and thus at peace with myself, not on the basis of any rightness or goodness that I can myself acquire, but by laying hold of the perfect rightness and goodness of God and humbly accepting His forgiveness for my own wrongness and badness. If I truly lay hold of God and accept the forgiveness He offers, I am released from the burden of the guilt of my sin, but I am at the same time given the only authentic secret of power over sin. All remedies for sin which carry us no further than merely setting our teeth to do good deeds which are still distasteful to us, and to avoid bad ones which are still alluring, are in the nature of quack prescriptions. The true secret is revealed to us only when something happens to us which begins to make evil ways distasteful and God and good desirable. Yet it is important that we should note the word *begins*. As I have already said at some length, few Christians, even after they have accepted the release from the guilt of their sin offered by God in Christ, ever do much more than make a beginning with the living of a holy life. Sin still retains a powerful hold over their wills, though it is no longer the old strangle-hold. And to suppose that we can ever, within the conditions of the present life, attain to perfect holiness of disposition is to endanger once again our grasp of the Christian salvation by cherishing a refined form of one of those very illusions which originally rendered our minds so inhospitable to it. That is why theologians have always been careful to distinguish what they called the state of grace from a state of glory. Here is what our old Scottish standard, the Westminster Confession of Faith, has to say about it: 'When God converts a sinner, and translates him into the state of grace, he freeth him from his natural bondage under sin, and by his grace alone enables him freely to will and to do that which is spiritually good; yet so as that, by reason of his remaining corruption, he doth not perfectly nor only will that which is good, but doth also will that which is evil. The will of man is made perfectly and immutably free to do good alone in the state of glory only.'[1]

But, as we have seen, the illusion that we can attain personal perfection in our own life is not the only illusory hope which has rendered men's minds inhospitable to the Christian Gospel; there have also been various illusions as to the possible future of our planetary history as a whole. Modern man has often seemed to be strangely satisfied with the basic conditions of his earthly situation. I should venture to forecast that when future ages look back on the unbelieving literature of the seventeenth, eighteenth, and nineteenth centuries, and compare it with almost any other literature that the world has produced, they will find nothing about it more striking than its *smugness*. It is indeed true that in its latest manifestations, at the end of the nineteeth century, such smugness took revenge upon itself and encouraged a reaction towards hopelessness, as in the Shropshire Lad and that other lad from Dorset. But if I were to mention also Ibsen and Nietzsche, it would then be clear that we

1. Chapter ix, 4–5.

were at the beginning of that most modern of all movements, to which I have already referred, of 'humanism turning into its own opposite', as it has now finally done in the Nazi paganism. Nevertheless the mark of modern unbelieving man as a whole is that he has felt astonishingly much *at home* in his earthly surroundings. He has taken a cheerful view of the prospects of the race and of the future of human history, staying his soul upon the promise of the further 'evolution' of the human individual, the continuous upward progress of civilization, or perhaps the confident expectation of a completely revolutionized order of society – a communist Utopia beyond the class struggle or something else of that same general kind. Where such hopes remain unchastened by the cold touch of reality, there is little prospect of the Christian Gospel recommending itself to men's minds, and any wordy defence of it is likely to be quite useless.

It is doubtful whether any who stay themselves with such hopes have ever faced up in a sufficiently realistic way to the simple fact that 'here we have no continuing city'.[1] Yet no philosophy of life is worth a moment's consideration which is not founded on the full realization that all human life inevitably comes to an end. This is something that all the great philosophers have well understood, while the little philosophers have often almost deliberately shut it out from their minds. 'Men are in danger of forgetting', wrote the greatest philosopher of all, 'that they who rightly practise philosophy study nothing else than dying and death.'[2] And the second greatest took the conception of *the end* as the central principle of his philosophy, thus leading up to the philosophic maxim *respice finem* – 'Look to the end'. A distinguished contemporary German philosopher, Martin Heidegger, though himself an atheist, has commanded the respect of a wide circle of students by taking this maxim far more seriously than other atheists have done. The leading principle of his philosophy is that of the *horizons*, as he calls them, within which human life has to be

1. Hebrews 13 : 14.   2. Plato, *Phaedo*, 64.

lived and which delimit the possibilities open to it. The final horizon is death – the death of the individual, but also the final death of society – which is therefore described as 'the last outstanding possibility which is at the same time the end of all possibilities', and which both includes and limits the other possibilities of human existence; it is 'the iron ring round existence.' Man, says Heidegger, feels his way outwards from himself to this horizon of death and then, feeling his way back again to himself, endeavours during the return journey to assess the possibilities that still remain open to him. The essence of human life therefore lies in the exploration of possibilities in view of the last outstanding possibility which is the end of all possibilities. Human existence is in its very nature 'existence towards death', though most men are not courageous enough thus to take full account of the horizon of death, and lead therefore what Heidegger calls 'an untrue existence'.[1]

Such also is the Christian view. At the very heart of Christianity there lies the tragic realization (a) that all human and earthly things must come to an end, and (b) that they must come to an end *before* they are made perfect. Our earthly pilgrimage is but a torso –

a watch or a vision
Between a sleep and a sleep.[2]

It strives after what it can never possibly reach. It is guided by an immortal light that can never be held in its own mortal hands. That is in itself a negative realization, yet the very negativity of it is quite vital to the Christian outlook on life. Christ came preaching a Kingdom that was not of this world, and all outlooks which find the kingdom of their dreams within this world, whether in the individual life or in the order of society, whether in the present or in the distant future, are directly

1. *Sein und Zeit*, Dritte Auflage, Halle, 1931.
2. Swinburne, *Atalanta in Calydon*.

contrary to the Christian Gospel. The first condition of a true attitude to life is the clear knowledge that it offers no prospect of the final attainment of heart's desire.

Yet if for this reason we should forsake or modulate our heart's desire, we should be guilty of an equally grievous error. Of the few things I know, there is nothing that I know with a clearer and more immediate conviction than that I must not be *satisfied* with anything that is less than *perfect*. Here is a region in which I am not permitted to cut my garment – my spirit's festival dress – according to my cloth. Whoever refuses to accept this rejects the foundation stone of the spiritual life of man. Alas, that it should be a stone rejected by so many builders!

> In my youth I set my goal
> Further than the eye could see.
> I am nearer to it now –
> I have moved it nearer me.[1]

We seem then to have only two choices open to us. We have to choose between despair and faith. On the one hand there is the final defeat of the hopes by which alone we can live; on the other there is the looking forward to some kind of transcendent realization of these hopes beyond the boundaries and possibilities of this present life. This is a conclusion which robust thinking cannot possibly escape. It is the conclusion which has been reached by all robust thinkers, Christians and unbelievers alike. I have no respect whatever for your timid mediating illusionists – 'the trembling throng whose sails were never to the tempest given';[2] but for those who have been brave enough to look the bleak prospect in the face without blinkers I entertain very high respect indeed. They may not be in possession of the true solution, but at least they permit themselves a clear-sighted view of the terms of the problem.

At the heart of the Christian faith there lies not only the

1. Rebecca McCann, *The Cheerful Cherub.*
2. Shelley, *Adonais.*

negative conviction that the perfect kingdom can never be realized in this world, but also the positive conviction that it nevertheless is real and will be realized. This is what Jesus Christ came to preach. 'Now after that John was delivered up, Jesus came into Galilee, preaching the gospel of God, and saying, The time is fulfilled, and the kingdom of God is at hand: repent ye, and believe in the gospel.'[1] Such is our summary of the first Christian sermon. 'For here we have no continuing city, but we seek one to come.'[2] The pilgrimage to which I would invite you is a believing pilgrimage towards this Celestial City. When Bunyan's pilgrims were progressing towards this same city, you remember that they came first to the Delectable Mountains from which 'they thought they saw something like the gate, and also some of the glory, of the place', but their hands shook as they looked through the perspective glass which the shepherds gave them, so that they could not look steadily or see clearly. Perhaps there are some of us who have stood on these Delectable Mountains and got no further. Later on the pilgrims met a man coming towards them, who had passed the mountains but had now turned back from the city. His name was Atheist and he asked them whither they were going. Then follows this dialogue in the matchless style of a writer about whom George Saintsbury said that he had 'one of the greatest gifts of phrase – of picking up the right word or the right half-dozen words – that man has ever had'.[3]

Christian. We are going to Mount Zion.
The Atheist fell into very great laughter.
Christian. What's the meaning of your laughter?
Atheist.   I laugh to see what ignorant persons you are, to take upon you so tedious a journey, and yet are like to have nothing but your travel for your pains.

1. Mark 1 : 14, Revised Version.   2. Hebrews 13 : 14.
3. *A Short History of English Literature*, p. 514.

Christian. Why, man! do you think we shall not be received?

Atheist. Received? There is not such a place as you dream of in all this world.

Christian. But there is a world to come.

Atheist. When I was at home in my own country, I heard as you now affirm; and from that hearing went out to see, and have been seeking this City these twenty years, but find no more of it than I did the first day I set out.

Christian. We have both heard, and believe, that there is such a place to be found.

Atheist. Had not I, when at home, believed, I had not come thus far to seek; but finding none ... I am going back again, and will seek to refresh myself with the things that I then cast away for hopes of that I now see is not.

Then said Christian to Hopeful, his companion, Is it true which this man has said?

Hopeful. Take heed, he is one of the Flatterers; remember what it hath cost us once already for our hearkening to such kind of fellows. What! no Mount Zion! Did we not see from the Delectable Mountains the Gate of the City? Also, are we not now to walk by faith? ...

Christian. My brother, I did not put the question to thee for that I doubted of the truth of our belief myself, but to prove thee, and to fetch from thee a proof of the honesty of thy heart.

Hopeful. Now do I rejoice in the hope of the Glory of God.

So they turned away from the man; and he, laughing at them, went his way.

Current discussion of this matter inclines to turn on the question of the immortality of the individual soul, and more often than not even confines itself to that question. But that is not the primary question in the Bible at all. The Old Testament has next to nothing to say about it, and the thought of the New Testament, though it everywhere extends to it, nevertheless takes its departure from a very different point. The Bible is not concerned with the individual merely as an individual, nor with his merely individual end and destiny. The Bible is concerned with the community, and with the end and destiny of the community; and is concerned with individuals only as members of the community, without whom there would be no community, though it is both profoundly and tenderly concerned with them when regarded in this light. Current thought is often content to regard the Kingdom of God as a realm which is always there, above this world, and into which individuals pass singly when their earthly biographies come to an end. But the Bible is concerned in the first place not with the end of individual biographies but with the end of history. Christianity has always taught that there can be no full glory for the individual until the glorified community comes at last into being, when at last the society of the redeemed is complete. The Bible as a whole consists of nothing so much as of what we should now call a philosophy of history.

At an earlier point in our discussion this Biblical philosophy of history was set in contrast with other philosophies of history, and one thing that emerged was that it takes the temporal process of things much more seriously than any other philosophy that had previously been promulgated. For the first time the process of events on earth was regarded as leading up to a final glorious consummation – a consummation that is the end of history in the sense both of completing and of transcending it. Eternity completes time, yet is no mere continuation of time. It is not more of the same but something unimaginably different. The question is not, as so often nowadays, one of survival, but of glorification. It is not a question of continuing the race but of attaining the goal and possessing the prize.

Something unimaginably different – that is what the Bible

always says. 'Eye hath not seen, nor ear heard, neither have entered into the heart of man, the things which God hath prepared for them that love him.'[1] Yet there are some pages of the Bible which do apparently describe in great detail the joys of the Celestial City. John Bunyan describes them too, and so do many of our most beautiful hymns. We hear of gates of pearl and streets of shining gold, of city walls garnished with jasper and sapphire and other precious and semi-precious stones, of crowns and candlesticks, and of a great multitude wearing white robes and bearing palm-fronds in their hands. But St John the Divine saw it all in a vision, and that other John of Bedford saw it in a dream. None of it, of course, is to be understood literally. It is not to be read as we read history, still less as we read the newspapers, but much more as we read poetry; for it is the fruit of the inspired imagination of the saints. Yet though we may go wrong by taking it as future history, we can go even more grievously wrong by refusing to take it at all. Here are the verses with which Bunyan concludes his book:

> Take heed also that thou be not extreme
> In playing with the *outside* of my Dream;
> Nor let my figure or similitude
> Put thee into a laughter or a feud.
> Leave this for boys and fools; but as for thee,
> Do thou the *substance* of my matter see.
>
> Put by the curtains — look within the veil,
> Turn up my metaphors — and do not fail;
> There, if thou seekest them, such things thou'lt find
> As will be helpful to an honest mind.
>
> What of my dross thou findest there, be bold
> To throw away, but yet preserve the gold.
> What if my gold be wrappèd up in ore?
> None throws away the apple for the core;
> But if thou shalt cast all away as vain,
> I know not but 'twill make me dream again.

1. 1 Corinthians 2: 9; Isaiah 64: 4.

And it is true, I think, that if we had not this wealth of celestial imagery provided for us, we should have to make sorry shift to dream it for ourselves.

What then of the individual's place within this heavenly Kingdom? When this question is asked, we notice that the Biblical authors first understand it with reference to those who will still be living on earth, when the end of history comes and the Day of the Lord dawns. Such of them as on earth have been true pilgrims will then pass into glory. But what of the generations that have already passed away and are now sleeping the sleep of death? In the ancient world the sleep of death never meant *extinction*, though nowadays that is the meaning often read into the phrase; the dead were conceived to be still in existence in an underworld–Hades or Sheol–though their existence was of so inert a kind as fitly to be described as a sleep. What then of the pilgrims who are thus asleep? This was the last question to be asked. The Old Testament has hardly anything to say about it, and the earlier parts of it nothing at all. However, in the period between the Testaments it came to be most actively canvassed, and the New Testament provides us with a clear answer. In what is probably the earliest of all the New Testament documents St Paul writes: 'But I would not have you to be ignorant, brethren, concerning them which are asleep, that ye sorrow not, even as others which have no hope. For if we believe that Jesus died and rose again, even so them also which sleep in Jesus will God bring with him.'[1]

Many of the further questions that we should like to ask are not answered for us by the New Testament or, where they are answered, it is in a highly symbolic and poetical way. But one thing is clear from its first page to its last – that all true pilgrims who meanwhile had died will rise again to share equally with the saints of the final generation in the things which eye hath not seen, nor ear heard, neither have entered into the heart of men to conceive. To know that is to know enough.

1. 1 Thessalonians 4: 13–14.

> I know not where His islands lift
>   Their fronded palms in air;
> I only know I cannot drift
>   Beyond His love and care.[1]

Can we believe this? Is it reasonable confidently to cherish such a hope? To this my first answer must be that it would be quite unreasonable to cherish either this hope or any hope at all apart from belief in God. Indeed, I have gone further, and have argued that our minds are little likely to be open to the entertainment of the Christian teaching either as to present salvation or as to final glory until we have first purged them of all romantic illusions as to what man can do in his own strength. But if we do believe in God, then it seems to me that no *further* act of faith is here demanded of us. Christian faith does not consist in believing a number of unrelated things, but in surrendering ourselves to a single act of trust in the God and Father of our Lord Jesus Christ. If we do that, then the other things follow, and among them this: 'In my Father's house are many mansions.'[2]

For to the narrower question whether it is reasonable to believe that the God and Father of our Lord Jesus Christ should by His almighty power receive into His heavenly Kingdom the souls He has redeemed through His beloved Son, I must reply by asking whether it would not be highly unreasonable to doubt it. The question is simply as to what the Christian faith implies in regard to the status and value of the individual human personality. Are we to think that individual human beings do not matter in God's eyes? I would put it to you that this is the very last doubt that should be raised in our modern minds, since it is on the Christian conviction of God's love for the least of these Christ's brethren that the whole of the Christian ethic is founded; and the Christian ethic — that is, the Christian way of treating others — is the one part of Chris-

1. Whittier, 'I bow my forehead in the dust.'
2. John 14: 2.

tianity of which something survives in practically every modern soul except Hitler's soul and those of others like him.
'Take heed that ye despise not one of these little ones'[1] –
even atheistic Bolshevism seems, in its championship of the
oppressed classes, to be not completely unaffected by the influence of these words. It is from Christianity far more than
from any other source that we have learned to value the individual human personality – a fact which is all the more significant because Christianity values the individual personality
only in relation to the beloved community of the Kingdom of
God. Yet it seems clear that we cannot hold to the Christian
ethical teaching about personality while rejecting the Christian view about its status in reality. You cannot be a Christian
in your moral principles and a Buddhist or a Nazi or any other
kind of pagan in your religion. If you try, you are experiment-
ing with an explosive mixture, and either your Christian moral
principles or your pagan religion will soon come to grief; and
though I hope for the latter result, I fear the former. I fear the
day will come when you will argue, as Hitler (who often names
the name of God) has apparently already argued, that 'if the
divine righteousness may lightly "scrap" the individual, human righteousness may do the same.'[2] If you do, you will be
arguing validly, and you can escape the conclusion only by
changing your premise.

This is the rock on which all modern substitutes for the
Christian belief in eternal life are likely to suffer eventual ship-
wreck within the minds of men of good will. You cannot be a
Christian in your ethics without being a Christian also in your
eschatology. You are unlikely in the long run to remain
staunchly Christian in your conduct of the present life, if you
refuse the Christian hope of life eternal. Every one of the substitute views involves the disparagement of the individual soul.
The doctrine of progress does this flagrantly, and so does the

1. Matthew 18: 10.
2. B. H. Streeter in *Immortality: an Essay in Discovery*, p. 85.

conception of the immortality of influence according to which men live again only in the minds of others 'made better by their presence', and so do all doctrines of an earthly Utopia. None of these take sufficiently serious account of those who perish by the way. The same objection applies with even greater force to the frequent tendency, manifest in so many of our contemporary high-brow, or perhaps rather 'middle-brow', novels and volumes of verse, to trifle with some vague quasi-Buddhist doctrine of 're-absorption', according to which our individual personalities sink back at last into the great Impersonal Spirit which is put in place of the Christian God. A reversion to the ancient Indian eschatology is far too likely in the end – for in the end logic usually prevails over the inconsistencies and eccentricities of opinion – to eventuate in a reversion to the ancient Indian ethics. Either the individual counts or he does not. If we think it right that he should not count for God, are we likely to go on believing that he should count for his fellow mortals?

14

Traveller's Joy and Pain

> BUT the slow watches of the night
> Not less to God belong.

So the hymn reminds us.[1] Our argument has been that the first condition of a true attitude to life is the knowledge that it offers us no prospect of the final attainment of heart's desire; but we must now add the second condition, which is that we should not on that account disparage the degree and kind of opportunity with which it actually does present us. The sober estimate of the possibilities of earth which lies at the root of all Christian wisdom finds proper issue neither in any despondency regarding present accomplishment nor in any relaxation of present activity, but rather in the better direction of our efforts and the wiser employment of our time. A French historian has claimed that such has actually been the result in Christian history. 'It is', he writes, 'the theologies of the enslaved will which have saved liberty; it is the theologies of salvation by Another than man which have saved human morality; it is the theologies of renunciation of the world which have saved man's mastery over the world; it is the theologies of man's renunciation of himself which have saved human personality; it is the theologies that preached love towards God alone which have saved love towards all men; it is the theologies of eternal predestination which have saved progress — even political and social progress; it is the theologies of heteronomy which have conferred on man an autonomy so fully master of itself as to be master of all else; it is the theologies that said "God is all, man nothing" which have made of man a force, an energy, a power incomparable and

1. F. L. Hosmer's 'Thy Kingdom come! — on bended knee.'

divine!'[1] There may here be some tendency to over-statement, yet it is a claim which I believe to be capable of large substantiation.

The truth is that an exaggerated otherworldliness is almost as remote from the true Christian attitude as is our modern secularism itself. I have known some men and women who had no thoughts for anything but the end of the world, and I have known others who had no thoughts for anything but this present life; and I know not which were the farther from the authentic Christian temper. Our business is of course in the present, and in the present only. 'We then as workers together with Him', says St Paul, 'beseech you also that ye receive not the grace of God in vain.... Behold, now is the accepted time: now is the day of salvation.'[2] An intemperate optimism which refuses to recognize the limitation of our human powers can do nothing but defeat its own ends. The chastened optimism which finds in present opportunities of blessedness the earnest of an eternal blessedness meanwhile beyond our reach, and yet does not decline or disparage them because they are no more than an earnest – such a temper is much more likely to be enjoined with true perseverance and to succeed in 'getting things done'.

Once again, then, as at an earlier point in our discussion, we find ourselves attempting to occupy a position somewhere between perfectionism on the one hand and the renunciation of all sanctification on the other. I am willing to confess that the reconnoitring of this intermediate position is the most delicate and difficult problem with which I am faced in my own personal life. I am at one moment tempted so to rely upon God's forgiveness as to expect in myself no growth in grace this side the grave nor any present abatement of my continued sinfulness, while at the next I am tempted so to rely upon certain

1. E Doumergue, *Jean Calvin*, Vol. IV, '*La pensée religieuse de Calvin*,' p. 39 f.
2. 2 Corinthians 6: 1–2.

observed possibilities of such growth as to cease to place my hope of salvation in divine forgiveness alone. The same contrary temptations threaten us in the wider sphere of the life of society. We are tempted on the one hand to transfer to the earthly scene those hopes of a perfected community which the New Testament allows us to entertain only with reference to the transcendent Kingdom of Heaven, or on the other to renounce altogether the hope of an improved earthly society as well as our efforts to bring it about.

But just as I am not permitted to say to myself that because God accepts me 'just as I am', I need not meanwhile expect to become other than I am, but must wait for the perfection promised to the saints in glory, so it is not permitted us to say that because perfect society can exist only in heaven, we need meanwhile expect no help from God in the endeavour to attain a better state of society on earth. We must accordingly consider the nature of the help God actually gives us in our efforts to set in order our earthly life and society.

As for myself, I could have no possible heart for such efforts if I did not believe that some divine help was available towards their accomplishment; and I am sure that most men, if they search their hearts, will have to make the same confession. We in this country are, as I write, engaged in desperate conflict with a powerful and unscrupulous foe. We believe we are fighting for the right and against the wrong. Never, we believe, have men defended a better cause or been faced by a more naked display of the powers of evil. There is nothing of which we are more assured than that it is our duty to oppose the unprincipled tyranny of Hitler's 'new order in Europe' and to work with all our might towards the establishment of an order of a radically different kind. Yet I believe there is scarcely a man among us who would have any heart for the struggle if he believed that we had nothing to rely on but our own strength and skill. I find that most of the men about me are very confident about the final outcome of the war, and I often ask myself where this confidence is based and how it is to be psychologically analysed. It is clear to me that it is hardly ever based upon calculations of military strength alone. Nearly always there is in it something much deeper, some latent and almost 'instinctive' assurance that because our cause is a righteous one it *must* prevail in the end. Very often, no doubt, this instinctive assurance is interpreted in the sense of a belief in a 'universal law of progress' such as Herbert Spencer formulated. I have already contended that there is no such law, but my present point is that those of our contemporaries who still believe in it are obviously relying, like Matthew Arnold, on *something*, 'not ourselves, which makes for righteousness'. They feel that in fighting for the right we are allying ourselves with something much greater and more powerful than ourselves, so as in some sense to have the very nature of things on our side. Not all are willing quite to say with Thomas Carlyle that 'the great Soul of the world is just', but most will at least say that a nation which gives itself over to unprincipled wickedness is working for its own eventual downfall, while on the other hand it must be true in some sense, if not quite as the Hebrew proverb meant it, that 'righteousness exalteth a nation'.[1]

Yet the instinctive feeling of confidence which is thus variously interpreted by the victims of modern uncertainty is actually nothing but the tattered relic of an older and more robust belief in God. The Bible everywhere encourages us to believe that those who work for righteousness are allying themselves with His almighty power and can count on His support, while those who work towards evil ends are His enemies and have His power against them. All through the wars of the Old Testament it is not Israel that is spoken of as winning the battles but God. 'So God subdued on that day Jabin the king of Canaan before the children of Israel.'[2] And when the battle was over Deborah sang in her famous song that 'the stars in their courses fought against Sisera',[1] who was Jabin's commander-in-chief. This song is possibly the oldest piece of Hebrew literature now extant, and it is significant that the collection in which it was originally preserved was entitled 'The Book of the Wars of Jehovah'.[2] Deborah's words find echo in the remainder of the stanza already cited from one of our own hymns:

> And for the everlasting right
> The silent stars are strong.

How endlessly the Old Testament may be quoted to the same effect! 'Some trust in chariots, and some in horses, but we will remember the name of the Lord our God.'[3] 'Through thee will we push down our enemies; through thy name will we tread them under that rise up against us. For I will not trust in my bow, neither shall my sword save me.'[4] 'The Lord of hosts proclaims, Israelites and men of Judah are trampled down together; their captors hold them fast and will not let them go. But theirs is a strong champion, his name the Lord of hosts; he will take their part, and daunt the Babylonians, that the world may live at peace.'[5] 'Except the Lord keep the city, the watchman waketh but in vain.'[6]

What right had the Israelites, and what right have we, to believe that God is on our side? The solemn answer must be that we can count on having God on our side only so far as we are on His. The question is not really whether God is allying Himself with us, but whether we are allying ourselves with God; but whenever we do ally ourselves with Him, working towards His ends and putting ourselves in line with His purpose, we have the full assurance of His providential help. The true principle for the guidance of our belief in providence is given us in the words of our Lord, 'But seek ye first the king-

1. Judges 5 : 20.   2. See Numbers 21 : 14.
3. Psalm 20 : 7.   4. Psalm 44 : 5–6.
5. Jeremiah 50 : 33–4.   6. Psalm 127 : 1.

dom of God, and his righteousness; and all these things shall
be added unto you.'[1] Such is the ground of our confidence –
that if we are engaged in His service, He will give us all the
help we require. 'Be not therefore anxious ... for your heavenly Father knoweth that ye have need of all these things.'[2]

Yet it is precisely at this point that our Christian faith is subjected to the greatest of all strains. It is terribly difficult to fit
the facts of life as we experience them, and still more perhaps as
we observe them, into this exalted Christian view of God's
providential ordering of the world. Not that it is any easier to
fit them into a doctrine of evolutionary progress such as Spencer's or into any other of the modern alternative readings of that
something, not ourselves, which makes for righteousness – of
that I am convinced. It is recorded in *The Later Years of
Thomas Hardy* that the first Great War 'destroyed all Hardy's
belief in the gradual ennoblement of man, a belief he had held
for many years.... He said he would probably not have ended
The Dynasts as he did end it if he could have foreseen what
was going to happen within a few years. Moreover, the war
gave the *coup de grâce* to any conception he may have nourished
of a fundamental ultimate Wisdom at the back of things.'[3]
Hardy was at least wiser than some of his contemporaries in
realizing that the facts which threaten our trust in God place
at least as great a strain upon any kind of belief in a natural progress of the human race. And now in the midst of another and
even more dreadful war the same problem recurs. If God's
purpose is a purpose of righteousness, why does He allow evil
to prevail? Why does He so long delay His help, suffering us
to endure so many defeats and retreats and disasters? Why
does He permit the cruel horrors of the Jewish persecution
and the German concentration camps, and the brutalities
wreaked by the fury of our enemies upon the Poles and

1. Matthew 6: 33.
2. Matthew 6: 31–2, Revised Version.
3. P. 165.

Czechs? And why must we all suffer the bitter pains through which we are passing now?

We should in no wise be afraid of putting these questions boldly, but should rather be suspicious of any form of faith which hesitates to put them boldly, since such hesitation, where it exists, may very well be due to a lack of sensitiveness to the sufferings of others than ourselves. It is perilously easy for the more fortunate among us to take a complacent view of those ills which have never touched our own case. As the French saying has it, '*Nous avons tous assez de force pour supporter les maux d'autrui.*' Much healthier, despite its element of wilful extravagance, is the reported saying of the saintly 'Rabbi' Davidson that when he looked out on the world the first thing to strike him was not the sin but the suffering.

The Biblical authors are always very bold in putting this question to God. There is one jeremiad which begins, 'Thou art always in the right, Eternal One, when I complain to thee; yet I would argue this with thee – Why do bad men prosper? Why are scoundrels secure and serene?'[1] Very many of the psalms argue thus with God. 'In God we boast all the day long, and praise thy name for ever. But thou hast cast us off, and put us to shame; and goest not forth with our armies. Thou makest us to turn back from the enemy ...'[2] The whole book of Job is such an argument, quite prodigious in its boldness. Yet it is to be noted that Job, no less than Jeremiah, both firmly believes in God and firmly believes also that God is 'always in the right'. For those who have not this faith there can be no problem of suffering. If the world be not ruled by One who is both sovereign Wisdom and sovereign Love, there would be no reason to expect any disposition of things that favoured either our own legitimate interests or the interests of righteousness in general. Atheists need not at all wonder that wicked men should flourish like the green bay tree, while most of us salt our bread with tears. It is only men of

1. Jeremiah 12: 1, Moffatt's translation. 2. Psalm 44: 8–10.

faith who are surprised. Job does not know the answer to his problem, but he knows there is an answer. So he ends his long complaint by saying, 'Shall he that cavilleth contend with the Almighty? ... Behold I am of small account; what shall I answer thee; I lay my hand upon my mouth.'[1] The phrase is half echoed by another and latter-day poet for whom the world's suffering had apparently ceased to be a problem, though it remained a burden –

> But men at whiles are sober
> And think by fits and starts,
> And if they think, they fasten
> Their hands upon their hearts.[2]

But Job laid his hand upon his mouth.

To cease believing in God would certainly be a way out of our problem, if it were available; but it was not available for Job and it is not available for me. I have already said that only he truly believes in God who cannot help believing in Him, and such was Job's case and is mine. God is not to be evaded; His is an authority and a Love that will not let us go. 'When I think my bed will ease me, my couch will soothe my complaint, then thou scarest me with dreams, thou appallest me with nightmares.... Let me alone, my life is frail and fleeting! What is man that thou dost make so much of him, fixing thy mind on him, punishing him every morning, testing him moment by moment? Wilt thou never take thine eye off me, or leave me for a second? If I sin, what harm is that to thee, O thou spy upon mankind!'[3] So speaks Job; and for me too the problem is how to reconcile two realities neither of which I find it possible to ignore, the reality of God and the reality of the world's pain.

Yet it is not as if the situation thus brought about were wholly opaque to our minds. There are two sets of

1. Job 40: 2, 4.   2. A. E. Housman.
3. Job 7: 13–20, Moffatt's translation.

facts that undoubtedly carry us part of the way towards a
solution.

In the first place, a large part of the world's pain is quite
manifestly due to the world's sin; and so far as we can actually
see this to be the case, the pressure of the problem is palpably
lessened. I know that many of the troubles that weigh most
heavily upon myself are the result of my own disobedience
and wickedness, and these I cannot honestly use as material for
complaint against God. I know also that many of our present
national distresses are the result of our national disobedience,
and as to these also I must 'lay my hand upon my mouth'. I
should have to confess that in my own case it is my sins that
have done most to make my misfortunes unbearable. A misfortune that befalls me in the course of doing my duty, and
when I am in the way of obedience, does not hurt and oppress
me at all in the same way as a misfortune which I have 'brought
upon myself' or which I think may be a divine punishment of
my own sin. It is the latter kind of trouble that is for me the
hardest of all to bear. I can conceive no greater torture, for instance, than the knowledge that a mortal disease which I had
contracted, such as would put an end to all my work and bring
bereavement and straitened circumstances to my family was
the result of my own dissipation of my bodily powers. And
even as it is, I am often haunted by the feeling that if only I
were always in the way of obedience, thinking little of myself
and much of God's glory and of the work He has given me to
do, such troubles as I have to endure would not harass me as
they do. Yet those troubles which I do know to be the result
of my own imperfect obedience, though they thus harass me
sorely, do not at all tend to remove the thought of God farther
from my mind, tempting me to disbelieve in Him, but tend
rather to make the remembrance of Him more inescapable
than ever. It is indeed reasonable that this should be their effect on me since, as we have seen, it is not the cases in which
sin leads to disaster that have placed strain upon men's trust

in God but rather the cases in which disaster does *not* appear to follow sin, so that the wicked man flourishes. It would be impossible to believe in God in a world in which no sequence of sin and suffering were perceptible at all. 'To judge from the threnodies of the modern pessimist,' wrote James Martineau in his somewhat flamboyant yet wonderfully eloquent way, 'he is chiefly impressed by the *miseries* which vice and wrong produce. Would he then prefer that they should produce happiness? or would he have it make no difference to the eternal well-being of mankind whether greed and licence prevailed or disinterestedness and purity? ... Sin being there, it would be simply monstrous that there should be no suffering, and would fully justify the despair which now raises its sickly cry of complaint against the retributory wretchedness of human transgression.'[1]

The second fact helping us towards a solution is our ability to recognize a disciplinary value in some suffering quite apart from the question whether the sufferer has brought it on himself by his own sin. This, like the other, may be said to be part of the spiritual common sense of our race. Our poetry is full of it and it is part of the meaning of tragedy, both Attic and Shakespearian. *Pathos mathos*, says Aeschylus – 'suffering is education'[2] – and Shakespeare:

> Sweet are the uses of adversity
> Which, like the toad ugly and venomous,
> Wears yet a precious jewel in his head.[3]

It is felt that some suffering is a necessary part of any environment in which character can be formed. The man whose life runs in too smooth a groove is likely to grow up lacking manliness and decision. Moral fibre can be formed only when some resistance is offered, when there are hazards and obstacles to be

1. *A Study of Religion*, Vol. II, p. 99 f.
2. *Agamemnon*, 177.
3. *As You Like It*, Act II, Scene i.

overcome.[1] Shakespeare says again that extremity is the trier
of spirits,

> That common chances common men could bear;
> That when the sea was calm all boats alike
> Show'd mastership in floating.[2]

Robert Browing in his more romantic way bids us

> Then welcome each rebuff
> That turns earth's smoothness rough,
> Each sting that bids not sit nor stand, but go!
> Be our joys three-fourths pain!
> Strive, and hold cheap the strain;
> Learn, nor account the pang; dare, never grudge the throe![3]

But it would be tedious to quote other equally familiar poetical
expressions of the same sentiment.

This common element of human insight is raised to its
highest potency in the New Testament understanding of the
sufferings of Christ; and that in two ways. For the first it will
be sufficient to quote that single New Testament author who
tells us that God made the Captain of our salvation 'perfect
through suffering',[4] who says of the Captain Himself that
'though he were a Son, yet learned he obedience by the things
which he suffered',[5] and who adds for our sakes the reminder
that 'If ye endure chastening, God dealeth with you as with
sons.'[6] But the life of Christ is marked not only by the brave
and believing endurance of suffering, but no less by the brave
and believing effort to relieve it. The four Gospels are very

1. A comparison may be drawn with art, as in Théophile Gautier's
famous lyric beginning,

> Oui, l'œuvre sort plus belle
> D'une forme au travaille
>   Rebelle,
> Vers, marbre, onyx, émail.

2. *Coriolanus*, Act IV, Scene i.
3. *Rabbi Ben Ezra*, vi.   4. Hebrews 2: 10.
5. Hebrews 5: 8.   6. Hebrews 12: 8.

largely a record of a ministry of healing. 'Then Jesus answering said unto them, Go your way and tell John what things ye have seen and heard; how that the blind see, the lame walk, the lepers are cleansed, the deaf hear, the dead are raised, to the poor the gospel is preached.'[1] It is in such loving services as we can render to our suffering neighbours, in the redress of wrong, in the relief of poverty, and in the battle against disease that life offers us its greatest opportunities of discipline.

Now if we could see that all our suffering were such as to fall under one or other of these two heads, if we could see that each calamity was *either* brought upon ourselves by our own avoidable misdeeds *or* was, as Browning says in the context of the lines already quoted, 'Machinery just meant to give thy soul its bent', then the problem of suffering would be solved for us. There would still indeed be possible certain more ultimate questionings as to why it should thus be decreed that character should be attainable only by so difficult a road, or why God should allow men to fall into sins that bring such terrible suffering in their wake; but the more limited question which we are now considering would have been fully answered. Yet it is not so answered. There remains much suffering in the world that appears to us to be the result of no human sin and to go beyond all requirements of the building up of character.

The mystery then remains; but it would be well to ask whether we should not expect it to remain. Ought we not to be suspicious of explanations of the scheme of things entire that make every part of it quite clear to our limited human vision and transparent to our finite minds? Have not the poets also taught us that mystery has, paradoxically, its necessary place in any illumination of things that can satisfy the spirit of man —

> Like aught that for its grace may be
> Dear, and yet dearer for its mystery.[2]

Truly it would be but a 'sorry scheme of things entire' that

1. Luke 7: 22.   2. Shelley, *Hymn to Intellectual Beauty*.

such as I could wholly understand and justify from this little stance that I occupy in time and place. This also is part of the spiritual common sense of our race, though only in the New Testament has it been worked up into a satisfying conception of faith, which is here understood as a childlike trust in the God and Father of our Lord Jesus Christ.

Therefore when the sufferings of the world seem most mysterious to me, when natural disasters like famine and earthquake wreak apparently insensate destruction on men and women who are no more deserving of them than the rest of us, when innocent children are tortured and deformed by horrible diseases, we must remind ourselves that even such things as these might be more intelligible to us, were the infinite pattern of existence a little less hidden from our eyes. And again when righteousness seems to await in vain its promised vindication, when those who seek the Kingdom of God and His righteousness do *not* have the other things added unto them, when the cause of justice languishes and the armies of the oppressor go from strength to strength and from victory to victory, we must remind ourselves that we mortals are hardly in a position to dictate to the immortal God just how and when He should make His triumph manifest. We are confident as to the final outcome of the present turmoil, because we are confident in God. But that does not mean that we know *when* He will give us the victory or even *that* He will give us the victory in the sense we have in mind. What we do know is something both less and more than this – 'we know that all things work together for good to them that love God, to them who are called according to his purpose'.[1] To rest confidently in the ultimate assurance is one thing, but to possess any foreknowledge of proximate events is quite another. The grand march of history is on a scale far beyond the compass of our finite minds, nor is the long-term strategy of God ever such as we can understand in advance, though we may sometimes be granted the wisdom

1. Romans 8: 28.

to see its justification in retrospect. Already God in His loving wisdom has deemed it right to discipline our nation severely. We have suffered sore disasters and defeats; and it may be that there are still disasters in God's will for us before we are allowed to see the triumph of the right. We are not even given the certain foreknowledge that He will grant us victory in the present series of campaigns at all. 'The end of the war' may not mean the same thing to us and to God; His divisions of time and its events are not ours. No doubt it would be otherwise if our cause and His were entirely coincident, but this they never are. We know, perhaps as surely as we know anything, that our cause is more in line with His purpose than are the designs of our enemies, yet we know that it also is infected with the limited perspectivity of human wisdom as well as tarnished by the admixture of many sinful desires. The real support of our spirits thus lies not in any certain foreknowledge of the shaping of events but in the firm assurance that God is all the time working for and with those who are working for Him.

When all is said, however, the deepest tragedy of life resides, not in those sufferings which seem to fall in such different measures on different men, but in such conditions of earthly existence as are common to us all. The ultimate sadness is that nothing lasts; that the bloom so soon disappears from all things that are young, that the vigour of maturity is so short-lived, while age brings weariness and forgetfulness and decay such as presage the oblivion and corruption of the grave. This is why 'our sincerest laughter with some pain is fraught.' To call to mind the care-free days of youth, to see the friends of youth disappear one by one from our earthly company with hopes only half fulfilled and work only half done, and to know that no task of our own can ever be completed nor any joy held in possession for more than a few fleeting years – this is our great heaviness of heart. And for it I know no healing, nor for the problem of suffering any final prospect of solution, save as we are able to share St Paul's faith when he cries, 'For I reckon that the sufferings of this present time are not worthy to be compared with the glory which shall be revealed in us.'[1]

About our human suffering, therefore, Christianity has ultimately the same thing to say to us as about our human sin – it repeats to us the story of the life and suffering and death and resurrection of Jesus Christ. The solution of both problems is somehow in that story. We there learn of One who spent His life in the relief of the sufferings of others and left His disciples an example that they should follow in His steps. We there learn that in Him 'we have not a high priest which cannot be touched with the feelings of our infirmities; but was in all points tempted like as we are, yet without sin',[2] having 'learned obedience by the things which he suffered.'[3] There we learn also that 'through the obedience of one shall the many be made righteous',[4] that His sufferings were for our sakes and were an instrument of blessing not only to Himself but to the whole sinning and suffering world of men. And there we learn finally that, having suffered and died on our behalf, 'now is Christ risen from the dead, and become the firstfruits of them that slept',[5] and that 'if so be that we suffer with him', it is 'that we may be also glorified together.'[6] Therefore, 'beloved, think it not strange concerning the fiery trial which is to try you, as though some strange thing happened unto you; but rejoice, inasmuch as ye are partakers of Christ's sufferings; that, when his glory shall be revealed, ye may be glad also with exceeding great joy.'[7] The contribution which the Gospel makes to the problem of suffering is in enabling us thus to relate our own little lives to the incarnation and passion and resurrection and exaltation of the eternal Son of God.

1. Romans 8 : 18.
2. Hebrews 4 : 15.
3. Hebrews 5 : 9.
4. Romans 5 : 19, Revised Version.
5. 1 Corinthians 15 : 20.
6. Romans 8 : 17.
7. 1 Peter 4 : 12–13.

15

Invitation to Church

FROM first to last, we have said, the interest of the Bible is focused on the community. In the earlier parts of Old Testament history this community appears to be identified very simply with the Hebrew nation, so that religious and patriotic aspiration are not distinguished from one another, but are directed towards the same object. The promises of God were promises made to the nation and the believer's hope in God was a hope for the future of the nation; nor could salvation have any meaning except in terms of membership of the nation. Something of the same sort is true of all ancient civilizations; loyalty to the gods and loyalty to the tribe or nation were not two loyalties but one.

The outstanding contribution made to the world's thinking by the great prophets of Israel was their realization that, in a world of sinful men and nations, the two loyalties cannot really be identical. They did not doubt that Israel was God's chosen people and that to it the promises had been made, but it was clearly revealed to them that these promises were not unconditional and that the Hebrew nation was no longer fulfilling the conditions but was in many ways giving herself over to apostasy. They were therefore led to distinguish between the nation as a whole and that 'faithful remnant' of it which still persevered in God's worship and service, and they taught that in this remnant would the promises be fulfilled. Thus was born into the world the distinction between religious and national community, since the dissociation of religion from nationality carries with it at least the possibility of men of all nations sharing the same religion.

Yet it is most important to realize that what here emerged was essentially the possibility of a new type of community, and not the possibility of a worship of God apart from all community. The prophetic revelation was of a true Israel within the Israelite nation and eventually extending beyond it. And this is the conception which is carried over into the New Testament. In the figure of Christ, who is 'a son of David' and 'a rod out of the stem of Jesse', the destinies of the true Israel are gathered up and brought to fulfilment, so that we who are followers of Christ are the heirs of the promises made by God to Israel. The community of Christian believers is spiritually continuous with the 'faithful remnant' of the Hebrew people. It alone is now the true Israel, elect of God, and called to be His witness among the nations, while it looks forward in faith to the establishment of the 'new Jerusalem'. Just, then, as in ancient Hebrew times religion meant membership in the Israelite community, so now Christian religion means membership in the Church of Christ.

Unless we understand this, we understand nothing about Christianity – or nothing as it ought to be understood. Christianity is essentially a community affair. This does not mean that it is not at the same time a personal affair; on the contrary, it is just because it is a community affair that it is a personal affair; for it is only in community that personality can be born and developed. Moreover, not all kinds of community are equally conducive to the growth of personality; for personality arises only within communities which have in them what I must call, though not very euphoniously, some potentiality of universality. A herd of deer, a pack of wolves, a school of porpoises no doubt enjoys some sense of community, but the individual deer and wolves and porpoises are not persons, because they have no sense of the universal bearing of their individual lives. The philosophers define a person as an individual which is conscious of itself in relation to universal being.[1] We shall not therefore be surprised to learn that personal religion, as we now understand it, came into the world at the same time as did universal community. I have no doubt at all that *something* of both had been in the world as far back as history can reach – some sense of a private relation between the individual soul and God, and some sense of a distinction between the nation as a human corporation and the nation as the vehicle of fellowship with God; but it was with the partial dissociation of religion from nationality in Israel, and with the consequent dawning conception of a universal religious community, that there emerged that remarkable development of personal religion which characterizes the later or post-exilic parts of the Old Testament, such as the Book of Psalms.[2]

Of these twin closely-connected revelations – the revelation of the possibilities of personal religion and the revelation of universal community – the Christian Church is now the heir. Christian religion is a relation between the individual soul and God, but it is a relation that can be realized only within that universal community which is the Church of Christ. This

---

1. e.g. Paul Tillich, *Religiöse Verwirklichung*, p. 169: '*Persönlichkeit ist dasjenige individuelle Sein, das sich zum universalen Sein erhebt.*' The classical definition of Boethius, which was standard throughout the Middle Ages, runs: *Persona est naturae rationabilis individua substantia –* 'A person is an individual substantiation of rationality.' But if we believe with the Middle Ages that only by means of our reason can we apprehend the universal, it matters little whether we speak of rationality or of universality in our definition.

2. 'Opinions as to the dating of the *Psalms* have undergone considerable changes in the twentieth century, and most scholars today would attribute a much larger number of the psalms to the pre-exilic period than did their predecessors. Many of these have the appearance of being the utterance of individual souls.... Yet the view is rapidly gaining ground that where such "individualistic" psalms are to be assigned to the pre-exilic age, they either present the community under the guise of an individual, or they form part of the regular ritual carried out in certain forms of legal process whereby Yahweh was invoked.' – Oesterley and Robinson, *Hebrew Religion: Its Origin and Development* (1930), p. 302.

means that I cannot be a Christian all by myself. I cannot retire into my own shell or into my own corner and live the Christian life there. A single individual cannot be Christian in his singleness. This does not mean that Robinson Crusoe ceased to be a Christian when he was cast upon his lonely island. On the contrary it was there, according to Defoe, that he began to be a Christian. 'In the Morning I took the Bible, and beginning at the New Testament, I began seriously to read it, and impos'd upon myself to read awhile every Morning and Night. ... I threw down the Book, and with my Heart as well as my Hands lifted up to Heaven, in a Kind of Ecstasy of Joy, I cry'd out aloud, *Jesus thou Son of David, thou exalted Prince and Saviour give me Repentance!* This was the first Time that I could say, in the true Sense of the Words, that I pray'd in all my Life; for now I pray'd with a Sense of my Condition, and with a true Scriptural View of Hope founded on the Encouragement of the Word of God; and from this Time, I may say, I began to have Hope that God would hear me.'[1] But Crusoe makes it clear that he could not have been a Christian on his island if he had had no previous association with the Christian Church before he went to sea, and had not had his Bible with him. Such Christian life as he could lead on the island, which though it was a real was far from being a full Christian life, was possible to him only because he could unite himself in faith with the universal Church of Christ, as revealed to him in the Bible and in his recollections of his Christian upbringing.

The case of Crusoe thus leads us somewhat deeper into the understanding of the nature of the universal community of faith which is the Church of Christ. Had Crusoe been an Israelite of pre-exilic days, he could not have worshipped God on his lonely island. He would have sat down and wept, as the first Hebrew exiles sat down and wept by the rivers of Babylon,

1. Defoe, *Life and Adventures of Robinson Crusoe*; entry in Crusoe's journal for 4 July 1660.

and cried, 'How shall we sing the Lord's song in a strange land?'[1] The early Hebrew conception of religion had, like all other early conceptions of it, been a strictly national and territorial one; but, more than anything else, it was the experiences of the Babylonian exile that were God's instrument for leading them to a wider and more spiritual view. 'There men of faithful souls went into Mesopotamia believing that they had left Yahweh [that was their name for their God] behind them. Their great discovery was to be that they were mistaken. They had not left Yahweh behind them; He was with them in Babylonia.'[2]

The Christian Church, then, is neither a local thing nor a human thing, but is universal and divine. It has nothing to do with place or race, nor is it an association created by men for their own purposes. Had it been any of these things, Crusoe could not possibly have been a member of it on his island. The Church is a divine society, created by God Himself; a society to which men are elected, not by any human vote, but by the grace of God; a society whose one condition of membership is faith in God's forgiving love. It is indeed a human society in the sense that its members are men and women, but it is a divine society in that its Head, on whom all its life depends, is the Son of God.

We speak very easily and familiarly nowadays of being a 'member' of this or that society. It would be difficult for me to count the number of clubs, associations, committees, and so on of which I now am or at one time or another have been a so-called 'member'. But we ought never to forget that this usage had its origin, as it still has its only full and real meaning, in the Church of Christ. The Church was the first society of which men spoke of themselves as being members, and when it was first used by St Paul this must have seemed a very

1. Psalm 137: 1–4.
2. Oesterley and Robinson, *Hebrew Religion: Its Origin and Development*, p. 291.

startling, and even extravagant, manner of speech. The great Apostle tried to explain the nature of the Church to his first converts by saying that it was Christ's mystical *Body*. Christ had once been manifest in the flesh and had had a body of flesh and blood of His own which was the vehicle and instrument of His intercourse with men. But this body had been broken and hanged on a tree, and now Christ must have another body as the vehicle and expression of His ever-living Spirit. The immensely solemn and moving thought which St Paul suggested to his converts was that we who are Christians are the limbs and organs of this mystical Body. We are Christ's hands and feet, His eyes and ears and mouth, through which He now continues to do His work in the world. 'For as we have many members in one body, and all members have not the same office; so we, being many, are one body in Christ, and every one members one of another.'[1] 'For as the body is one, and hath many members, and all the members of that one body, being many, are one body: so also is Christ. For by one Spirit we are all baptized into one body, whether we be Jews or Gentiles, whether we be bond or free; and have been all made to drink into one Spirit. And whether one member suffer, all the members suffer with it; or one member be honoured, all the members rejoice with it. Now ye are the body of Christ, and members in particular.'[2]

We are limbs of Christ, St Paul says, and at the same time limbs one of another. The two statements are of equal importance. It is only in Christ that we can enjoy full community with one another, and it is only in our togetherness with one another that we can enjoy full communion with Christ. Each statement deserves some further consideration. Let us take the second first.

At an earlier point we saw that to the individualistic rationalism which has characterized so much of the thought of recent centuries there was nothing in the Christian way of salvation

1. Romans 12: 4 f.   2. 1 Corinthians 12: 12 f., 26 f.

that presented a greater stumbling-block than what we may call its historical particularity. Such individualistic rationalism wanted the way of salvation to consist of a body of general ideas which was accessible to the solitary thinker in every time and place; but that salvation should be of the Jews, that to one people alone should the precious knowledge in the first place have been entrusted, that their obscure history should alone be supremely sacred and their little bit of earth the Holy Land and their literature the Holy Writ, that one particular Man should be the Son of God and the only Saviour of mankind, and that accordingly the saving knowledge was accessible only to those whose ears were reached by the rumour of His appearing – all this appeared to be a grave mismanagement on the part of divine Providence. Yet perhaps its very purpose was to confound this same individualistic rationalism, and to make it impossible for men to meet with God and to love Him without at the same time meeting with and loving one another. God has apparently done everything He possibly could, short of exercising actual compulsion upon our wills, to prevent us from making our religion a private luxury – and yet we still try to make it a private luxury! He has had resort to every legitimate artifice to have us unite with our brethren when we unite ourselves to Him, so that our piety could never be made to seem an escape from our social responsibilities – and yet we *have* made it such an escape! For what more could He have done than so to order things that men can find salvation only by betaking themselves to one place, where they are bound to meet one another – to the hill called Calvary; by encountering there a single historical figure – the figure of Jesus; by listening to the selfsame story; by reading in the same Book; by praying the same prayers in the same Name; by being baptized into the same fellowship and partaking of the same sacred Meal – 'all made to drink into one Spirit'; by drawing in fact their whole spiritual sustenance from the same unbroken tradition handed down from age to age? We must not indeed altogether ex-

clude the possibility of other revelations, either in the sense of
further disclosures of His will which God vouchsafes to individuals in special situations, or in the sense of divine leading
given to men and peoples who have not had the opportunity
of so much as hearing of the Incarnation. Even the Roman
Church leaves hospitable room for both these operations of
omnipotent divine grace. 'God, who wishes all men to be
saved', we read in Cardinal Gasparri's *Catholic Catechism*,
'grants to all the graces they need for obtaining eternal life,'[1]
and again, 'An adult person who dies unbaptized can be saved
... if, through the operation of God's light and grace, he is –
despite his invincible ignorance of the true religion – prepared
to obey God and has been careful to keep the natural law.'[2]
'The Church', writes the Roman theologian, Dr Otto Karrer,
'maintains that invincible ignorance or honest doubt of God's
existence does not exclude a heathen from receiving God's
grace, provided he lives according to his conscience, is re-
pentant for faults committed against it and is in his entire disposition a seeker after truth.'[3] 'According to St Thomas', he
says again, 'there is a "revelation" even in the absence of any
human agent to transmit a religious truth, if the mind of the
recipient is enlightened by a Divine illumination.... Obviously
where a historical revelation has been proclaimed this religious
attitude will take the form of an explicit acceptance of that
revelation as sufficient proof that it comes from God. Where,
however, a revelation thus clearly accredited is lacking, this
general faith must, as Mausbach truly urges, suffice by itself,
since the religious and moral disposition, the craving for
divine truth which gave it birth, "involves the willingness to
accept actual revelations".'[4] All this must be most cordially

1. 'Catechism for Adults', Q. 288.
2. *Ibid.*, Q. 162.
3. *The Religions of Mankind*, translated by I. A. Watkin (1936),
p. 236.
4. *Ibid.*, p. 242 f.

allowed – though non-Romans would wish to express it a little differently; but no part of it affects the truth that 'the ordinary means of grace' are of quite another kind. You and I owe all the knowledge of God that we have to our upbringing in the one tradition and our reception into the one fellowship of the Church of Christ, and the only way that is open to us whereby we should bring to others the blessings of that knowledge is by initiating them into the same tradition and receiving them into the same Church. Togetherness with one another is thus woven into every part of the fabric of the Christian worship of God.

'For where two or three are gathered together in my name, there am I in the midst of them.'[1] That word of Christ has sometimes been popularly misunderstood to mean that Christ was more likely to be present to small gatherings than to large ones, but of course its real meaning is more nearly the opposite – it means that Christ is more likely to be present to a community, however small, than to a single individual. What Christ would say is not 'only two or three' but 'at least two or three'. The promises of God are not given to those who think to serve Him in separation from their fellow men, or who try to love Him without at the same time loving one another. There is no surer way of allowing our spiritual life to sink into morbid unreality than by refusing to join with the congregation of the faithful. 'They were all with one accord in one place ... and they were all filled with the Holy Ghost.'[2]

Let us now look at our other statement, which was that only in Christ can we enjoy full community with one another. The new and in many ways tragic age in which we are now living is perhaps characterized by nothing so much as by a renewed hunger for the achievement of community. The age of rationalistic individualism is now for the most part behind us, and men are seeking new forms of solidarity in their social life. In one part of the world after another there emerges the spectacle

1. Matthew 18: 20.   2. Acts 2: 1, 4.

of men yielding up their individual liberty, including their liberty of thought, with apparent relief, gladly sinking their lives in the corporate life of this or that party or totalitarian movement. Those who saw anything of the life of the *Hitler-Jugend* in Germany before the war are familiar with one instance of this, but it is of course only one among many that might be cited. At first we were inclined to regard such movements with contemptuous indifference, but now at last we have been forced to recognize their immense power and vitality. What is it that has overtaken the youth of Germany, of Italy, of Spain, and of Japan, in a different way also of Russia, and in less startling form or degree of many other countries?[1] We thought it was a passing fever and we put it down to local and accidental causes; but I think we know better now. It is the returning desire for unity and community and conformity after the long reign of an amorphous heterogeneity and atomistic individualism, which had once been prized, but the taste of which has at last turned sour in the mouth. In one of his books Dr William Paton quotes the remark of one observer who exclaimed, 'I sometimes think that a great many of the younger people of today *have no sense that they belong to anything.*'[2] What we are now witnessing in the youngest generation of all is precisely the returning desire *to belong to something.*

The new solidarities which have thus emerged are of so perverted a kind as to be a menace to the whole future of the human race. Their perverseness is threefold. First, they demand total allegiance to a community which is not in its own nature total or universal. Second, and in consequence, they suppress and destroy personality by making the individual a subservient means to the ends of the community rather than in any true sense a member of it – for, as we have seen, it is out of universal community that personality is born. And third, these ends are in themselves for the most part evil ends and ideals; they are not Christian ideals, they are not even respectable pagan ideals, but rather the ideals of a latter-day pseudo-paganism — of what Professor Niebuhr has called 'synthetic barbarism'.[1] But perverse as it is, this new devotion to community is generating a fund of power which our recent atomistic individualism is likely to prove altogether too weak to resist and which, if it cannot be met by some communal solidarity of a purer and stronger kind, will soon have the game in its hands.

When we seek to muster our forces[2] in opposition to the Nazi and Fascist menace, under what contrary ideals are we to marshal them? We have all read many pronouncements on the matter, and roughly they all say the same thing: we are to oppose the new paganism in the name of humanity, justice, liberty, brotherhood, and the indefeasible value of the individual human soul. That answer is well enough, so far as it goes, but I am sure that it must go further. These indeed are the ideals of the Christian ages, or some of them, or at least they sound very like them, but in the Christian ages they were all deeply rooted in something bigger and grander, in something that was no mere ideal but an eternal reality. They were rooted in the love of God as manifest in Jesus Christ our Lord. No doubt they also drew something of their sustenance from classical antiquity — from Roman law and Stoic philosophy and other similar sources; but it was from a classical heritage that had been re-baptized into the spirit of Christ and had thereby been not only immensely fortified but also changed almost beyond recognition. It was Christ who taught us the indefeasible value of the individual soul. It was Christ who taught us the meaning of *fraternité* when He said, 'One is your

1. 'For the first time in history the barbarians which threaten civilization have been generated in the heart of a decadent civilization. The barbarism which threatens us is "synthetic" rather than genuine. Its vitality is not primitive but primitivistic. It represents a romantic effort to hide and to heal a decadence deeper than the disease from which the western nations suffer.' – R. Niebuhr, *Christianity and Power Politics*, New York (1940), p. 118.

2. 1942.

Master, even Christ, and all ye are brethren';[1] and St Paul when he said that 'we, being many, are one body in Christ, and every one members of another'.[2] Hence the doubt that keeps raising itself in my mind when I read these fine pronouncements about our ideals – in some of the *Oxford Pamphlets on World Affairs* or the *Macmillan War Pamphlets* or elsewhere – is whether these ideals have sufficient strength of conviction in them, or sufficient power of survival, in face of so powerful a contrary force, when they are no longer allowed to breathe their native air or draw daily sustenance from their original source.

The weakness of the ideal standards which we are today invoking against the threat of pagan totalitarianism lies not in themselves but in the fact that they are uprooted. So many of the pronouncements I have read have been written by men who are themselves thus uprooted. I have learned much from these men, and I know that I have much more to learn from them, yet I cannot think of them save as the Uprooted Ones, *les déracinés*. Or I think of them as Men of the Afterglow – a phrase which was, I think, first suggested to my mind by some sentences in which Principal Cairns, writing in 1937, spoke of the outlook of Dr Julian Huxley: 'Surely there is something defective in the outlook of any man who believes that we shall strengthen the cause of humanitarian progress by destroying faith in the sovereignty and providence of God. Has he really grasped the realities of the situation, measured the forces of evil that are against us, and the pitiful inadequacy of our merely human resources for even the earthly salvation of mankind? He and men like him seem to me to be living in the afterglow of a faith which they have believed themselves compelled to abandon, and seeing the world in hues that cannot last.'[3]

That is the real poignancy of the situation. These Men of the Afterglow, many of whom, as I say, have been or still are my

1. Matthew 23:8.   2. Romans 12:5.
3. *The Riddle of the World*, p. 164.

own honoured teachers and mentors, are seeing the world in hues that cannot last. 'We now', writes Dr William Paton in his latest book, 'behold the results of trying to maintain a political valuation of man which had roots in a religious understanding of him, after that religious understanding has been forgotten.'[1] Let me take but one instance of this from the War Pamphlets. Mr C. E. M. Joad writes as follows: 'Though I may have my doubts as to the immortality, I have none as to the importance, of individuals. Souls are souls even if their life here is transitory, and though they may not be immortal, it is none the less the business of the government to treat them as if they were. The announcement of the importance of the individual is, in my view, the greatest gift of Christianity to the world.'[2] These words are well meant and yet how pitifully weak, how preposterously inadequate! What comically little finger is this that we propose to shake against so powerful a foe! Is this to be all the battle-cry we give to our youth as we fling them against the Nazi hordes – *it is doubtful whether men are really immortal souls but you must treat them as if they were*? But I have already argued, when dealing with the question of man's eternal destiny, that we are little likely either to persuade others to believe or to continue ourselves to believe that the individual counts for his fellow-mortals, if we are content to think that he does not count in the eyes of the immortal God.

We are thus led to the inescapable conclusion that our ideal standards, fine as they may be in themselves, are likely to succumb before the pressure to which they are now being subjected, unless they drink again at the fountain from which they drew their life; and that, in particular, any merely individualistic version of them is likely to be powerless against the forceful appeal of totalitarian community spirit. Our only hope lies in finding another and nobler form of community which

1. *The Church and the New Order*, 1941, p. 152.
2. *For Civilization* (Macmillan War Pamphlets), 1940, p. 20 f.

will unite us in a stronger solidarity, and call forth a more deep-seated and passionate devotion, than even our foes can claim to possess.

Yet we do not really need to find it in the sense of inventing it. It has been found of God and founded by Christ; it is there before our eyes and the most we need do is to find it again. For the only community that is likely to be stronger than totalitarianism is a community which is universal, and there is only one such community – the Body mystical, the Church of Christ. In order to be universal a society must obviously be more than national and more than racial; and when we feel for the weak spot in the totalitarian front it is in its narrow nationalism and racialism that we think we find it and, for our victory over it, we count largely on the antagonisms thus aroused against it in the souls of other races and nations. But in order to be universal a society must also be *more than merely human*; and it is an equally serious weakness of totalitarianism that it demands my total allegiance for something that is not in its own nature total, for something merely human and earthly, that it 'deifies the state', whereas there is that left – often, thank God, very vigorously left – even in the souls of the Uprooted Ones which refuses thus to bow the knee to Baal.

The Church of Christ, and the Church of Christ alone, is both these things. In the mystical Body of Christ there is neither Jew nor Aryan, slave nor freeman, white nor coloured, but all are one. It is to be found all over the world and there is nothing else in the world that really resembles it. Britons and Frenchmen, Germans and Italians, Arabs and Hindus, Chinese and Japanese, Kaffirs and Zulus and Melanesians, men of every tongue and race and nation, are here found worshipping the same Lord, being baptized with His baptism, breaking bread at His table, praying as He taught them to pray, and trying to live as He taught them to live. They are all fallible men, there are among them many 'unhappy divisions', and nowhere can they claim to be worthy of the calling whereunto they are

called. Yet even in a time of wars and rumours of wars the
Christian Church, regarded merely as an association of men,
is doing more to bridge the gulfs that divide nation from
nation than any other association on earth. In a broken and
shattered world it still retains something of the character of a
universal community. But it is able to do this only because it
is more and other than an association of men, because its final
allegiance is to something beyond all differences of race and
colour and nation, something for which all such differences
are quite irrelevant, and because its treasure is in Heaven. It
can transcend our human relativities only because its obedience
is to the absolute and eternal God.

It is for the same reason that the Church can provide that
deeper grounding for our cherished ideals without which they
lack the substance and conviction necessary to make them
triumphant in the present crisis. Then, instead of standing
merely upon the abstract duty of being 'humane' to other
members of my own human species, I shall remember that for
these others Christ died. Instead of speaking abstractly of 'the
indefeasible value of the individual', I shall remember Him
who said, 'Take heed that ye despise not one of these little
ones',[1] and who, in the terms of His own parable, went out into the wilderness to find the one sheep which was lost.[2] And
not only my championship of *fraternité*, but also my championship of *égalité* will be subtly yet potently changed by being given this deeper grounding. It will no longer be 'I am as
good as you are,' but rather 'You are as good as I am.' It will
be an equality grounded in penitence rather than in self-
assertion. Likewise my championship of justice will be immensely fortified when I remember that its only foundation is
in the character of God – when I remember, in the eloquent
words of Dr Farmer's description of the prophetic teaching,
that the divine voice 'which condemns injustice is the voice of
Him who walks in thunder through the hills, and the plumb-

1. Matthew 18 : 10.   2. Luke 15 : 4.

line set against the immoralities of Jerusalem is an infinite perpendicular from the stars.'[1] The present chaotic state of human relationships throughout the world surely demands something better than a mere reassertion of such 'natural law' and such 'rights of man' – demands something more like a reassertion of the rights of God. It demands something better than mere justice, something more like Christian love. This does not mean that we can dispense with natural law and the codification of justice and the appeal to human rights; nor even that political action as such can ever express itself in other terms than these. What it means is that the men whose task it is to work them out in the field of political action are little likely to do so either with sufficient judgement or with a sufficiently staunch determination unless they are themselves all the time seeking refreshment at the deeper spring.

The weakness of our present situation is that men appear to be faced with a choice between two evils, on the one hand such a rediscovery of community as enslaves the individual to the state or race or nation, and on the other an individualism which is powerless to resist such totalitarianism both because it is weak in itself and because it fails to provide satisfaction for that returning hunger for solidarity which undoubtedly characterizes the youth of the present generation. I see no way out of this predicament save by the reintegration of the ideals, which even in our individualism we continue to cherish, in a community of a genuinely universal kind. Only in the fellowship of the Eternal can we escape *both* the totalitarian *and* the individualistic heresies. Dr Paton suggests that the reason why 'the British Commonwealth and the United States may justly claim to represent the true tradition of the West' is 'that they hold to the truth that the State is not autonomous but subject to a higher law.'[2] But, as he excellently shows, this higher law can be effectively vindicated, and can secure for itself a

1. H. H. Farmer, *The World and God*, p. 64.
2. *The Church and the New Order*, p. 143.

sufficiently steadfast devotion, only if it finds embodiment in a higher community. 'Mankind will not be able to establish a workable world until it realizes that on earth, as in heaven, it is not itself sovereign, but is only the mandatory of God.'[1] The Church of Christ is such a universal community: it amply provides the corrective for individualism, and at the same time delivers us from earthly totalitarianisms by directing our sovereign allegiance to God alone; while it further discourages us from taking precarious stand upon virtues which men can see that we do not possess, and inclines us rather to stand before men as sinners who have found forgiveness and who are called upon, not merely to defend their own rights, but to love and serve their fellows and to forgive as they themselves have been forgiven.

I hope, then, that I have provided sufficient reason why we should all seek the fellowship of the Church of Christ, there to rekindle our ideals and rehabilitate them in a solidarity that is stronger than all the solidarities of earth. There be many that have lately been saying of themselves, with Coleridge's Ancient Mariner,

> this soul hath been
> Alone on a wide wide sea.
> So lonely 'twas that God himself
> Scarce seeméd there to be.

But I hope I have given good reason why they should now decide, again with the Mariner,

> To walk together to the kirk
> With a goodly company.

> To walk together to the kirk
> And all together pray,
> While each to his great Father bends,
> Old men, and babes, and loving friends,
> And youths and maidens gay.

1. *Ibid.*, p. 163 f.

Index